Ezekiel Gilman Robinson

Christian character

Baccalaureate sermons delivered

Ezekiel Gilman Robinson

Christian character
Baccalaureate sermons delivered

ISBN/EAN: 9783337266301

Printed in Europe, USA, Canada, Australia, Japan

Cover: Foto ©Lupo / pixelio.de

More available books at **www.hansebooks.com**

Yours sincerely,
E. G. Robinson

[From a photograph taken at Providence, R.I., in 1882.]

Christian Character.

Baccalaureate Sermons

DELIVERED BY

EZEKIEL GILMAN ROBINSON,

President of Brown University from 1872 to 1889.

SILVER, BURDETT AND COMPANY.
NEW YORK ... BOSTON ... CHICAGO.
1896.

TO

The Members

OF

THE SUCCESSIVE CLASSES AT BROWN UNIVERSITY,
BEFORE WHOM THESE BACCALAUREATE
SERMONS WERE DELIVERED,

THIS VOLUME IS RESPECTFULLY INSCRIBED.

PREFACE.

THE following sermons are collected and given to the public in response to the wishes of many friends. They vary in length and completeness according to the varying ability of the reporters to seize the rapid utterances of the speaker; for, with one or two exceptions, they were prepared for publication from newspaper reports. But the shortest and most imperfect of the series present the leading thoughts and the progress of the argument. The editor has not, of course, felt at liberty to add to them, except at occasional defective points to complete the obvious intent of the speaker; nor has anything been left out, except occasional repetitions of statement or expression. Even these redundancies are sometimes left as characteristic of the preacher's more familiar public addresses; like the amiable defects of our friends, they will not be unwelcome to those who sought and valued his pulpit teachings.

The press of engagements as Commencement approached left to the President little time for writing out the theme selected for his annual discourse; and, indeed, it was not his custom to preach from notes. But it was only the form, not the substance of the sermon, which was left to the hazard of the occasion. The thoughts had been revolving and taking their logical place in his mind for weeks, perhaps months, before their utterance.

Coming to Brown University from a Theological Seminary where his classes were engaged on subjects of highest theological interest, he had to remember that he was speaking to younger men, as yet little exercised in the abstract forms of religious truth and inquiry. To this fact, and to the fact that he was specially addressing students whose attention he had been, for a year, stimulating by quick and trenchant question, is due the direct, personal style of the sermons. Only one or two of them exhibit the more restrained, formal qualities usual in discourses preached on special occasions.

They were "practically dialogued" — to use the expression of a brilliant lecturer[1] before the students of Columbia College — with the graduating classes. The sudden interruption of the argument by a swift application or searching question; the logic broken in upon by a pungent appeal or sharp thrust at the conscience, — these rapid parentheses show how purely practical the speaker's aim was. It was, in fact, in strong, simple terms, to impress upon the minds of each successive class, as his final word to them, the momentous truth that, in their future lives, the loftiest aims, the worthiest ends, the highest successes, were to be found, only and always, within the spiritual realm. As was said of Frederic Robertson, there was a "controlled passion" in his pulpit utterances which gave to them an intense reality and persuasiveness. Addressed primarily to young men, no one

---

[1] The Lord Bishop of Derry and Raphoe, of a series of Discourses published under the title of *Primary Convictions*.

could hear his vigorous words, poured forth warm from the deepest convictions of his soul, without a strong, sympathetic impulse toward a grander, purer life. The upbuilding of Christian character was the ruling motive of every discourse.

It is, of course, impossible on the printed page to convey an idea of the force, the *elan*, the magnetism of the spoken word. And yet, it may be permitted to add, that sermons subsequently preached in another city, characterized by the quiet authority of his years, and transfused with the glow of an ever-deepening faith and holy reverence, were, by many, accounted more powerful than those which swayed his Providence congregations. A deeper spiritual note, perhaps, was struck. As his day declined, the truth took on a more tender emphasis. The Christ whom he had always preached became to his faithful heart ever more and more a divine Friend, and, through His Holy Spirit, ever more and more his Light, his Strength, and his Inspiration.

HARRIET P. ROBINSON.

JULY, 1896.

CONTENTS.

	PAGE
CHRIST, THE WISDOM OF GOD. Sermon preached June 22, 1873	13
CHRISTIAN VIRTUE. Sermon preached June 21, 1874	28
THE RELATION OF RELIGION TO MORALITY. Sermon preached June 13, 1875	40
INWARD UPRIGHTNESS. Sermon preached June 18, 1876	59
NATURE AND CLAIMS OF MORAL LAW. Sermon preached June 17, 1877	78
THE SENSE OF DUTY. Sermon preached June 16, 1878	97
SCIENCE AND THE CHRISTIAN RELIGION. Sermon preached June 15, 1879	111
THE RIGHT AIM IN LIFE. Sermon preached June 13, 1880	131
THE SEARCH FOR TRUTH. Sermon preached June 12, 1881	149
THE SURE VICTORY OF FAITH. Sermon preached June 18, 1882	169
PERILS OF THE PRESENT DAY. Sermon preached June 17, 1883	184
FAITH AND SENSE. Sermon preached June 15, 1884	200
THE LIFE WORTH LIVING. Sermon preached June 14, 1885	208
TRUE WORSHIP. Sermon preached June 13, 1886	222
NATURE AND REVELATION. Sermon preached June 17, 1887	227
SERVING ONE'S GENERATION. Sermon preached June 17, 1888	235
GOD GLORIFIED IN CHARACTER. Sermon preached June 16, 1889	243

BACCALAUREATE SERMONS.

CHRIST, THE WISDOM OF GOD.

Christ . . . the wisdom of God.
1 CORINTHIANS i., part of the 24th verse.

SOME explanation of this universe is the instinctive demand of the human intelligence. It is a demand whispered at the dawning of consciousness. It grows in emphasis with the growth of years. It ceases only when the shadows are settling around us. The answers to this demand are now denominated, not, as in the text, "wisdom," but "the love of wisdom" or philosophy. The sum of these answers constitutes the sum of human philosophy. Some kind of solution of the origin, the laws and methods of whatever is, must be given; and philosophies of every description we therefore have, — the philosophy of the mind, the philosophy of mechanics, the philosophy of politics, — the philosophy of whatever is in this universe. But, as Socrates long ago intimated, and as Plato still more emphatically asserted, the grand philosophy is "the summation of man," — to tell what man is, whence man came, and whitherward man is bound. Paul tells us in brief phrase that the true philosophy is not that of Greece. But "the true philosophy," says the apostle, "is Christ;" philosophy in every age is the measure of a people's intelligence, the index of the height to which they have ascended; and not only of the intelligence of a people, but of every individual. Your philosophy and my philosophy is simply the measure of your and my intellectual stature. It tells what is your solution of the facts of your own being; and according to the rationality of that solution, you determine the dignity of the mind which propounds the solution. If philosophy be the measure of one's truest manhood, equally true is it that Christian philosophy is pre-eminently that measure and test.

Philosophy proposes three grand questions: the facts of being, the laws of being, and the relations of being. Christ is said by the apostle to be in Himself the answer to whatever question philosophy can propound. Christ answers the questions which arise respecting the facts of our being, the laws of our being, the relations of our being. But mark the language: it is not the assertion of the apostle that the moral teachings of Christ are the true philosophy. You are not to distinguish between what Christ said and what Christ was. Human philosophers are clearly and broadly distinguishable from their philosophies. You must look not too narrowly into the personal history of even Socrates. But when Christ stood before men, Christ was what He said; He embodied the principles which He enunciated. Human philosophers propound their premises, and then elaborately reach their conclusions. Christ Jesus spake from Himself — no deduction, no borrowing from any preceding teacher, but, in His own significant words, "Ye have heard of old time that it was said thus: Verily, I say unto you." Men say that He spoke by intuition. Solve it as you will, what Christ said, Christ was. And thus it comes that Christianity requires a man to be what he believes and affirms. In this is the grand distinguishing characteristic between Christianity and any human philosophy. Human philosophy enunciates principles; you may adopt them, and remain unchanged. To adopt Christian philosophy is to become Christian. To be and to say are identical in Christianity.

Happily, then, the three questions which philosophy propounds to man, Christ answers, "Whence are we? Why are we here? Whitherward are we bound?" Human philosophy has never been able to give the shadow of an abiding answer. Judaism did not answer distinctly; it taught us something of God, but not clearly. Christ first gave to man the true idea of God as a Father. True, the poet in his imagination had said, "We are His offspring," but it was poetry, and a mere imaging. Christ taught that we are the children of God. You may call Him, if you will, a Jewish peasant, uninstructed in the schools; a man whose dialect and person betrayed His humble origin; "familiar, it may be," you say, "with the flowers and the sparrows;" but Christ taught you and me to find God in every object of this universe, and not the God of the Pantheist, but a personal God; so that out of every flower we hear a Father's voice saying, "I made this for you," and every sparrow saying to us that God watches over it. They are all familiar thoughts to us now; but they came from Christ. Christ made known to us not only the Fatherhood of God, as the controversialist will tell you, but Christ made

God personal, — among us, of us, caring for us, — brought Him into our homes, made Him speak to us in words we can understand, identified God with all that is beautiful and true in our nature, in our aspirations, in our thoughts.

Christ taught us, not only whence we came, but why we live. Manifold had been the answers of the philosophers. For the sake of the state, they said; the highest idea of man in the Greek philosophy was his identification with the state. The man, his property, his highest thought, were subjected to the one idea of the state. But when Christ began to tell man why he lived, and how to fulfil the design of his existence, language needed reconstruction. Search the Greek; the very meaning of the word "humility" is meanness. No Greek could understand what Christ meant by it. To the Greek, as in later days to Voltaire, it was "the grace of a whipped dog." So of "righteousness;" Christ gave to it a new meaning, and when He taught the dignity of manhood, the worth of virtue, individual responsibility, the words had new meanings given to them. And for the attainment of these personal attributes in their new meanings, man was required to live, and through them he was to fulfil the design of his existence.

So, in respect to the destinies of man, vague and uncertain dreamers there had been. What idea does the human philosopher give of futurity? Strip the future of everything that Christ has given us, and it is indefinite and uncertain. Christ Jesus has made it clear to men that to be immortal is to carry with us the results of this life, to carry with us all our garnered affections, all our achievements, all our precious thoughts, all our high aspirations; that to be, is to be in the future what we are now. Christ made it a fact to man that immortality is perpetuity of personal being.

Christ is the true philosophy as to the facts of our being; He is also the true philosophy as to the laws of our being. These laws had been guessed by men. Here and there, glimmerings of the truth had been granted. Wonderful had it been if no ray of light had come to the human intellect; if no Confucius had ever grasped an immutable truth; if no Buddha had ever laid hold of some fragment of the Abiding; over this broad earth our God has smiled beneficent, giving truth to this one and light to that, leaving no one in helpless gloom. But it was Christ that enunciated once for all, in simplest language, the immutable truths of being. He has announced them to you; he has announced them to me. Whence came this wondrous knowledge?—a knowledge that stands the test of every form of criticism. Look at these philosophies of the past. You know that each strove to determine what was immutable truth. Each had some glimmerings. We read to-day what we call Christianity in Plato. We gather here and there many a truth from the Stoic; many a truth from Epicurus, it may be; but after all, truth amid an accumulated amount of corruption which no human intellect can separate from the few truths scattered. Look at Christianity. Not a truth about it is lost. Point out, if you will, one solitary ethical principle taught by Christ that has been tested and found wanting. It is simply because Christ did not devise. He simply revealed. Christ drew aside the curtain and told us what is, and has made it to be forever true that the ethical principles which bind us here are simply the revelations of our own immutable being. So that when Christ tells us what is obligatory, He simply tells us what is immutable. And these ethical principles which Christ has thus taught, are to-day tested and found by every man to be adequate to all his necessities. Whatever may be your peculiarities of constitution, let these truths remain on your ear long enough to be sounded in the depths of your being. He who gave you your being has spoken to you in these revealed truths of Jesus Christ, saying to you what you are and what you must be, or perish.

Christ, then, is the philosopher or philosophy, in enunciating the immutable truths of morality. The morality of to-day, the morality of the centuries, is simply the morality of Christianity; all that which survives to-day is found in the Gospel of Christ.

But there is another question which Christianity propounds to us, and that is, the *relation* of man to the laws of his being and to destiny. Manifold are the answers. The philosopher of the past could merely throw in upon the great darkness of your mind the simply enunciated truths of moral obligation, and leave you to struggle with them in silence alone. Christ Jesus enunciated these truths, and when He enunciated them, said, "Come unto me, all ye that labor and are heavy laden, and I will give you rest." How familiar these words, how unmeaning to many, how inexhaustible to all who have pondered them — "Come unto me, all ye that labor and are heavy laden" (with the oppressing thought of your obligations), "and I will give you rest." This is the grand philosophy of Christianity — this is the relation of Christ to man. It is on this point that men have concentrated their minds, and it seems to me have obscured the simple teaching of Christ. We all know the mediæval theory; alas! that it still lingers among us. We all know how this has been repeated and incorporated in literature and hymns, that Christ Jesus lived and died, and by that death alone, once and for all, accumulated the merit which it is the special province of a delegated class of men to hand over to others; or, that the grand office of Christ in visiting this world was to offer Himself, simply that men, having wasted life, having degraded their natures, should by His merit be transferred forever to the place which God had provided for them. The salvation was a process of reckoning, an arithmetical process, a commercial transaction. It still lingers among us, and there are people who tell me that, if I am to be saved by Jesus Christ, must it not be by imputation, must it not be by reckoning. No, now and forevermore, no! God Almighty does not save men by reckoning, does not save men by causing us to look ever backward to a Christ that died once, and accumulated something which somebody is intrusted with, to transmit onward to us. Christ has delegated no man to stand between Himself and me. He who tells us that Christ is to be approached by His mother, or that Christ is to be approached by some specially delegated and consecrated person, tells us a lie, tells us what Christ Himself repudiates. "Come unto *me*," says Christ. So that salvation will be serviceable to me and to you, my young friends, only as you go to Him in your own weakness and helplessness.

This is our Christ, — God manifest in the flesh, and one of us, — as true and real a man as you, as true and real a man as I, with all the temptations and trials of man. Having put Himself into the position of one of our race, it was inevitable that He must die; and because He did die and triumph, you and I will triumph. And why? Not by trusting to what some one has told us has been accumulated, but by trusting to *Him*, — not to a dead Christ, but to a living Christ, — to a living, personal Christ, to-day here. Not a Christ hung upon a crucifix, not a wax image, not the Christ of a dogma, not the Christ of a mere creed. Let us, in the name of this abused Christ, arise up, and once for all away with whatever stands between us, whether it be dogma, whether it be creed, or whether it be Church or priest. I set before you that personal Christ who says to you, "Come unto me, all ye that labor and are heavy laden, and I will give you rest." And Christ died for you, if you will trust in Him, but not without that trust. He died for no man that does not find Him to be a risen and exalted Saviour, — a personal Christ, and a personal salvation to him who desires His salvation. This, then, we understand to be the true philosophy of His personal relation to man. When it says that God is manifest in the flesh; when it tells us that Christ took our nature and bore our iniquities, died for our sins, — it tells us a fact, an immutable fact, — the fact that He does die for us if we put our trust in Him, but if we do not, he dies no more for us than if we never had been. But

He is yours, if you come to Him as one who has passed through this way of life, just such a way as every one of you must pass; you will have your temptation in the wilderness, you will have your struggle, you will have your garden where in your agony of soul you will be confronted with the devil. There is no other that can guide you in the wilderness; there is no other that can guide you in the garden; there is no other that can guide you in the time that shall come, when you must be either crucified in your thought, in your flesh, and in your spirit, when you must surrender up all but what God Almighty lays upon you, or sacrifice yourself; when you must either accept the crucifixion of selfishness, and lust, and evil desire, or must die the death of the doomed and abandoned. Let there be no trifling about this matter.

Law, we have said, is as immutable as the throne of God. Salvation is as free as the air to any man that will put himself into relation with Christ; and salvation is as impossible as the transformation of yourself into a Deity, unless you shall come into relation with some one competent to be an object of trust and a Saviour. Say, then, that Christ is to be your Saviour. Where else have you found one? I set Him before you as the true Philosopher of the method of human redemption, an atoning Saviour, who died for you, who died for me; one who died in obedience to an inexorable necessity; one whose agony in the garden, whose agony on the cross, you can solve by no empty theory short of this simple fact,— that having taken our nature, having put Himself into that vortex, He must either bear the great burden of our guilty being, and bearing it, rescue our nature, or sink forever.

You and I must find our trust in Him that hath conquered, or we shall be conquered.

Young men, I say to you now, that just as true as God rules, if you trifle with evil, if you sell yourself to temptation, just so true it is that you will die in hopeless agony, and reap as you sow. Nor is God's mercy thus impeached. It is impeached if any man tells you, "He is so gracious, He will forgive you." Alas, alas, God is not a being who has power to arrest penal consequences. Remember what we have here said: It is not in His power to arrest penal consequences. It is written in the very heart of your being, and you can realize your own nature lifted up, expanded, harmonized according to the idea presented in Christ Jesus, only as you come into relation with Him. Therefore, I commend Him to you as the Philosopher touching your relation to law, to God, to yourselves, and your destiny.

Here I am not unaware of the objections that will present themselves at once. You will ask: "Is not Christianity questioned in our day?" "Is it not confronted by men whose opinions are enunciated with all the assurance that accompanies the enunciation of Christian truth on the part of its adherents?" Undoubtedly, just in proportion to the clearness and emphasis with which Christian truth has been enunciated, has been the counter enunciation of opposing sentiment. It is not mere legend that tells us that when our Lord began His career upon the earth, the devil confronted Him. Just in proportion to the clearness of truth in every age will be the declaration of an opposing thought. It is the nature and the history of man and of human opinion.

The opposers of Christianity revive all of the opinions that have been tried in the ages of the past. What do they propose? Do they offer you anything which, having been tried, is found to be superior to Christianity, either in its answer respecting your origin and destiny, or respecting the laws of your being, or respecting the methods of attaining to the realization of your ideal? What is it that these opponents of Christianity contemplate? Is it a higher standard of human being? Is it a higher character? Where does one of them exhibit it? What, then, do they offer? It is not a higher civilization. When they tell you that Christianity has obstructed the progress of the race, ask them for the proof. Doubtless there has been perversion. The great wonder that the Church presents to the world is, that long ago it was not sunk in the depths of the sea by its professed friends. I confess that there is nothing that so strikes me with amazement, as that Christianity has survived the errors, the superstitions, the debasements of its adherents. It is of God that it has been able to carry such an oppressive load of human error and superstition. When, therefore, we set before you Christianity, do not mistake objections to the errors of its friends, for objections to Christianity itself. It is for this reason that I tell you that it is not to the professed priest, it is not to the professed claimant of divine prerogative; but it is to Christ that I commend you.

There is another form of objection to which I must refer. A strong weight of prejudice rests upon the minds of young men that the Christ of the Gospel is a person specifically belonging to the Church and to the Sunday, or at best to the occasion of the funeral service, when all else is gone. I commend no such Christ to you here to-day. That is the error which lingers among us, when certain persons stand among you, and claim a certain prerogative because they are dignified by the title of minister. I know of no title given by God or man other than simply the ability to do what Christ tells us, and that is, to explain the truth aright, and present, in one's own character, the doctrines of Christ. The only man whom God has called, whom the Almighty has predestinated to teach religion, is he who, in his own person, exhibits in some degree what Christianity requires; and who, by exhibiting, is competent, and authorized to teach it to others. It is not, therefore, the religion or the Christ that belongs to a specific class of men. The Christ of the Gospel is the Christ of the highway, the Christ of the feast, the Christ of the wedding, the Christ of the market-place, the Christ that is to be carried with you wherever you go. I warn you, young gentlemen, that whatever your office, you take Christ Jesus with you wherever you are. The one want of our time is a Christ in the counting-room, a Christ in the Legislative Assembly, a Christ in the court-room; not a Christ presented in the empty forms of perfunctory prayer; not a Christ that belongs to the church, shut up in it, to be presented to us only on the Sabbath day; not one to whom I am going to resort in whining petitions when I have to surrender up this life, — but a living, personal Christ, of whom, young gentlemen, you speak not in profanity, not in flippant language, but whom you will dare to avow when you stand before juries and courts, whom you will avow in your daily transactions with the world, in your homes, in society, always, everywhere. This is the error of our time, that we have separated our religion from our morality. We have a Christ for sacred days; a Christ for special occasions, — but no Christ to walk these streets and stand here among men. There is a sort of spirit in this day that taboos the man who dares speak of Christ on a festive occasion. No, no, friends, this has been our error; this has been our danger. This is the ruin of our times, that we have men who sit at the sacramental board and hold positions in the church, and yet stretch out their smooth palms and take bribes; who stand ever ready to legislate, and yet by their acts deny the Christ whose presence among the money-changers, in the market-place, everywhere, said, " Be honest; be open; be frank."

This is the Christ I commend to you, young gentlemen. Never be ashamed to avow yourselves as the followers of Him who was the ideal man. Why be ashamed to say, " I accept Christ as my pattern," because there is a lingering notion among men that you are only to call on Christ when you die, or when you are where the priest is? Our Christ is the Christ of all time, the Lord of the earth, the Light of men, not simply a Lesson for Sunday-school children, but a Mighty Power for stalwart men, whose glory it becomes, to stand up and say, each one, " I am a Christian." And let it be understood, wherever we are, on whatever occasion, that Christ is not the special property of the man known as the minister. I am almost ashamed, at times, to have men say, " You are a minister, are you?" Why a minister any more than you that call yourself a Christian? I claim no right to preach Christ from anything committed to me. No mortal man authorized me; no mortal man can. I speak of Christ because I trust in Him; He is our Light and Peace and Saviour. He is the "Wisdom of God," the Creator of this world, the Saviour of man, and I know of no other. Young gentlemen, this is the Christ that I want to commend to you, — the Wisdom of God. And I warn you never to be ashamed of Him. Oh! that any man ever dared to poison his lips by speaking His name profanely. If any of you have ever dared to trifle with that name, in God's name, I warn you to do so no more. Think of His dignity! Think of His humility! I can think of no higher thing than that. When you stand at the bar, or in the pulpit, as educated men, competent to guide, I beseech you to say, "before all men" "I have accepted Christ as my teacher; I accept Him as my example; I accept Him as the grandest man that ever stood upon this earth; I accept Him as the Divine Being come down from heaven." You need not be cringing; you need not be timid. I warn you against cant. It is death to all true manliness, to all true virtue; it is death to everything dignified and dignifying. But in simplicity, in manliness, in honor, in righteousness, say with Julius Müller, that if Christ were a mere ideal, that ideal would be worth dying for — that if He had never lived, it would be worth laying down your life to give to future generations the ideal of such a man. But He is more than that. He is with you always. Will you despise Him? Will you turn away from Him? Will you neglect Him? I offer Him to you to-day as the Infinite Wisdom.

I have spoken of the trouble you will have in life. Stern trial will come somewhere, and at some time. May you meet it manfully. May you dare to say " I accept this great Being as my Guide ; " and then, when the times come for you to lay down your lives, may the Father's smile rest upon you ; may you see Christ, and may you hear His voice saying to you, " Be of good courage. I have overcome." " I am the resurrection and the life." Young gentlemen, be Christians in the Christian sense. God be with you all.

CHRISTIAN VIRTUE.

Giving all diligence, add to your faith virtue.
2 PETER i. 5.

ACCORDING to the uniform teaching of Scripture, it is impossible for man without faith either to please God, or to pass through this life without final and fatal loss. It is accordingly insisted upon that whoever will be saved shall believe. Nor is this an arbitrary requirement. Faith is insisted upon in compliance with the necessities of human nature; for faith is the common principle on which everything human that is enduring or valuable is dependent. Society rests upon it. Without it government is impossible. Man, if faith ceases, ceases his exertions; and according to the strength of his faith are all his personal efforts. Faith is the informing principle of all character. A man, every man, is according to the objects of his trust.

The difference between Christian faith and the common beliefs of men is a difference between the object or objects believed in; the difference between faith and the common beliefs of men is also a difference between the qualities or attributes of the objects trusted, or believed in. Christian faith rests upon Christian objects and seeks Christian ends. It manifests itself in unmistakable products. These products are variously designated; for it is noticeable that the common language which Christianity now employs has been derived from varied sources, not from the Bible alone. Thus the language which it employs in designating the results of faith has been borrowed from other than Scriptural sources. Two not infrequent terms in our modern religious and philosophical language have come to us from the philosophers of antiquity. No terms in Christian literature are more commonly used than " morality " and " virtue." But " morality" is a word to which the Scriptures are at every point strangers. The word is foreign alike to the terminology of the Old Testament and of the New. " Virtue " is appropriated here and there incidentally, — most commonly in a meaning other than that which it had with the philosophers either of Greece or Rome. And yet the word in the text, more, perhaps, than in any other single passage, retains its ancient meaning, but purified and transfigured by the transforming power of Christianity. When we turn to the Bible, the words which meet us are "good works," " righteousness," " godliness," " holiness." These are terms which differ only in the point of view occupied by the speaker, from those two words which I have referred to as having come down from heathen moralists; between " virtue " and " godliness " — or, as it may be put, " god-likeness " — there is much of resemblance; and between what we designate as " morality," and what the Scriptures call " good works," there is the closest affinity. And when the word " morality " is understood in that sense which, through centuries of continued discussion, has come to be represented by it, then we say it embodies a genuine Christian thought, — but only because Christianity has adopted it, infused into it its own meaning, imparted to it something of its own life.

But the one word which is presented to you to-day is "virtue." "Add to your faith virtue" — not simply in the Roman sense of manliness; not in the narrower sense of courage; nor are you to understand by it any single virtue. Philosophers have discussed long and ardently the question, "what are the great virtues which constitute permanent and worthy character?" From Plato to our own day, what are called in technical language the "cardinal virtues," have been sought, but they are yet undetermined. Certain cardinal virtues are accepted by all. What is fundamental of the series is yet a disputed question, except by those who plant themselves upon the Christian basis, and receive their morality from Jesus of Nazareth. When, therefore, we speak of "virtue," let us not understand any one virtue. You may adopt, if you choose, the modern, common classification of the cardinal virtues, and say that they consist in fidelity, in justice (or justness), in temperateness, and in courage. But no one of these constitutes virtue, — no one, if you sever it from the others. The united four constitute, provided they are pervaded by an informing spirit, what our text and what moralists recognize as true Christian virtue; embodying all the single virtues, uniting them into one grand comprehensive, harmonizing spirit which gives to man courage to be faithful in his convictions, courage in subduing his natural tastes to the requirements of temperance, — and temperance in no narrow and technical sense, but temperance in that broad spirit which says to each taste and each appetite, "so far and no farther," — "temperateness" being perhaps a better term than temperance. So that underneath what is designated by the term virtue, you will understand "ability," — power to execute your convictions, ability to conform yourself to what you know to be right. It is not something assumed. It is not something fleeting. You might say it is like that which the athlete, from the severity of his regimen, and the protracted discipline to which he subjects himself, acquires, a sinewy, vigorous, supple strength, to do just that which he proposes to do. Or, it may be said, it is more than this; it is a subtile, ethereal power, penetrating the very fibres of the soul; uniting a man into one complete personality, by which what he sees to be right he does, by which what he is compelled to regard as right, he is able to do. This, then, is *Christian Virtue*, ever remembering it is "Christian" because it is derived from Jesus Christ, and is the result of the indwelling spirit of Jesus Christ.

Why seek to acquire Christian virtue, — such a presence and power and abiding ability; not one virtue, but all virtues so blended that a man is said to possess personal virtue? There are advantages in its possession. There are reasons why you should seek to make yourselves possessors of it.

First of all, it gives an unfailing protection, — a protection that envelops its possessor in a panoply which no weapon can penetrate. It surrounds him with a coat of mail which the dart of no archer can pierce; or, changing the image, it is putting within the man a spiritual force which comes forth spontaneously and invariably at the required moment. It is a spirit, a life, a power; and it is as a spirit, a life, a power, that it harmonizes and brings into a rounded wholeness, every attribute or quality of character. Thus its possessor can confidently confront the world, clad in an armor which no power can crush and no foe penetrate.

More than this, it gives to its possessor a constant peace and satisfaction. To him who possesses Christian virtue in the sense given to the term, there is a profound consciousness of security. It may be the result of outward trial; it is the result of repeated moral conflict, but once possessed, it is a conscious possession, — not vainglorious, not boastful, but an inward, silent, personal force. We are told that it is a pleasure to stand in conscious safety in a tower and witness the rush and rage of battle. It is a pleasure from a high cliff to look out upon the ocean lashed into fury by the raging winds. But there is no pleasure like that of mingling in the storm of moral conflict, consciously clad in an armor which is impenetrable, and which insures a certain victory. There is pleasure in the sense of security; but it is heightened into exultation when taking part in the fray, when confronting evil, when bearding the wicked in their dens. The man feels that righteousness is in him, that integrity is his, and that a Divine power rests upon him, because he has lost himself in the consciousness of that invisible and enveloping Presence that in using him, is charging his weakness with a Divine strength. Every man who, through painstaking and tears and supplications and prayers and conflicts, has acquired this sense of security, knows what I mean when I say that the possession of it gives a pleasure with which no honor of men, no earthly wealth, no other possible acquisition, can compare. He who has it dwells in the unbroken peace of God, — a peace which, in the language I have read to you, "passes all understanding."

Again, this virtue of which I have spoken, is an indestructible possession; not simply something covering him as with a cloak, but something infused into the very fibres of his spiritual being. This, then, is part and parcel of one's own identity. When that point is reached, it may be called *character*, if you choose; it is that which a man, having once acquired, can never be despoiled of. It is his own. He walks abroad in God's universe with an indestructible possession. So long as he exists, so long his virtue abides; and it abides with him, because it is something congenial, kindred, a component part of his own nature, a vital element in his own spiritual nature.

Nor need any man, with his technical, theological dialect, be disturbed when we say it is a righteousness imparted. It is not alone imputed, it is imparted; and that man who knows anything of true Christianity, knows that He from whom he receives righteousness and life is a Being of whom it is said, "He is in you the hope of glory;" and you are in Him, "your life is hid with Christ in God;" and "he that hath this hope in him purifieth himself," so that "as Christ is, so are they who are His." This personal virtue, then, is something which God, in His infinite wisdom, has actually imparted to man, as his own inalienable possession. It is said that knowledge shall pass away; of the various graces, that one and another shall cease; but that there is one which shall abide, charity, — charity which embodies all righteousness, which is only another name for, and is of the very essence of, virtue.

But the query arises, How is this Christian virtue to be acquired? Certainly not by any faith in abstractions, whether they be pantheistic or positivistic, nor by faith in the immutable in nature. These are virtues especially set forth in our day. There is a kind of ideal, stoical virtue, like the marble statue, — beautiful to behold but pulseless, inanimate. Is that the virtue to take the place of Christian virtue? You may acquire such. It is not difficult, but it is the virtue of the cynic, it is the virtue of the cold-blooded soul, from whom all sympathies have departed; but Christian virtue is that which takes man as God's creation, takes every instinct, every faculty, every endowment, every aspiration under its control, harmonizes, blends them all into the realization of the ideal man, — the perfect man in Christ Jesus. How shall you acquire it? I have said that much depends on your faith. If you are led on by an absorbing trust in some human end, it will stamp itself on your character, for every man becomes like the object of his trust; it will write itself in lines easily read of all men; it will be depicted in your countenance, show itself in your gait, and breathe in the very spirit that animates you. Such a lower end reveals itself in the whole course of a man's life; it can never lead to the virtue for which I am pleading. The virtue I mean is that derived by trust in Him who alone of all the beings that ever stood on this earth could be called "the perfect man," — Christ Jesus, the Ideal, the Real, — " God manifest in the flesh." And the virtue thus acquired by trust in Him may seem at first a faint spark which the slightest breath can extinguish; but once begun, God in His mercy protects it, cherishes it, feeds it, until it grows up into full life, "unto the measure of the stature of the fulness of Christ."

But the virtue of which I have spoken has been called "the virtue of the weak-minded." It has been said that it is not the virtue of the stout-hearted and heroic, but that it begins in penitence, in tears, in self-distrust. So it does; and there is no true personal virtue which has not this beginning; there is no other which bears the stamp of divinity, no other which its possessor can prove, no other which can survive the trials and dangers of this life.

> "True dignity abides
> With him alone who in the silent hour
> Of inward thought can still suspect and still
> Revere himself."

There is no virtue in this world which does not first of all begin in self-distrust, in self-humiliation, in self-abnegation. No man ever finds himself until, for the sake of the ideal and the real as illustrated in Christ, he shall have lost himself; and he who has lost himself for Christ's sake, finds himself the possessor of Christ's power, Christ's virtue, Christ's righteousness, — of a personal righteousness, which, given by God, is his own inalienable possession.

Young Gentlemen of the Graduating Class: You are gathered for the last time here in sacred service. I have attempted to set before you something of the value of Christian virtue and the method of its acquisition. Will you make it yours? There are other ends in life; they are numberless. They salute you on the street corner; they come borne to your ears on every wind. You are solicited on every hand to issues innumerable in life. There is the one still small voice that says to you, be true to yourselves, true to your religious convictions, true to your God; and, being thus true, in patience, in humbleness, in distrust of self, but in an immovable faith in God, you shall acquire a virtue that will support you in every change of life, that will survive when this world has passed away from your vision. Little will it be to the glory of any one of you, if at the end of your career the most that can be said of you shall be, "he did not violate the commandments of the moral law. He was neither a thief nor a liar, and he did not debase his high talents and his possessions to minister to his appetites and passions." In this age of venality and self-indulgence, this age in which betrayal of trusts is so common, it may seem something of praise to say of a man that he never betrayed his trust. But when you look far out into the future, when you think of all that God has intrusted you with, may He keep you from the dishonor of the merely negative praise that you were not debased and debauched, and did not defraud; rather, may you carry with you the consciousness of integrity, of an upright purpose, — a purpose which no allurement shall ever make you swerve from; a determination that, with God's help, you will do despite to every tempter, you will adhere only to honor, truth, and righteousness. If wealth comes, if honors come, be thankful; but let the one fixed and steady and unflinching purpose of your life be to make of yourselves noble men, — men to whom God has given the virtue that was in Christ, — the ability to follow your convictions, and power at all times and under all circumstances, to stand up with an open face, with a serene brow, and, looking into heaven, to say, with no vain boastfulness, " I thank thee, O God, that Thou hast kept me true and firm and steadfast. " That is worth all the honor of men. For what are the honor of men and the possessions of this earth in comparison with the possession of that which goes with you forever, and which God shall recognize as the stamp He Himself has put upon you?

I see opening from this place a lengthened road. Along it I see your hurrying steps in the great race of life. Now one and now another drops by the way to rise no more. You pursue your forward course more gravely, with diminishing numbers and slackened pace. A half century has sped, and only two or three of you are patiently, faithfully toiling up yonder hill. As you wend your way amid the familiar scenes, your frames bowed with the weight of years, your brows furrowed with thought and care, you turn and survey the past. Ah! may the gracious words, may the sweet charities which you have exchanged with one another in the last three days, ever abide with you as indestructible memories; may you know what it is to have lived honestly, never to have proved unfaithful to your convictions, never, in this age of venality, to have sold yourselves for name, place, or wealth. I adjure you, keep your spirits pure, and turn from the tempter in whatever form he may present himself.

And, above all, let me ask you to remember that this virtue of which I have spoken will never come to you, until your faith shall have rested in that One Being who alone is the Source of it. Let it rest there to-day, young gentlemen. You each have known what it is in childhood's simplicity to bow the knee before Him; and though you are now young men, you are not too old, and never can be, to bow in childlike simplicity at the feet of Christ, and ask Him to keep you and cleanse you from evil, and to strengthen you for the right, and to give you a virtue that shall be satisfied with no mere negative qualities, but a virtue like that acquired by men of old who were ready to lay down their lives for righteousness' sake. You may have despised the methods of the monastic periods, and you may have looked over the annals of the Puritans and said, "Alas! what a mistake, what misapprehension!" But they were all men of integrity, of patience, of self-sacrifice. And in this age of criticism, when we cast reflections on the past, and talk of the Christianity which so refines and civilizes and promotes the graces and industries of society, I warn you to remember that there is no virtue, there is no true piety, there is no true character, there is nothing worthy to be possessed, which is not to be possessed by that same spirit which led men in the past age of monasticism, in the age of the Puritan, in every age, to sacrifice self, to sacrifice ease, to sacrifice all indulgence to the one determined purpose to honor God. I charge you, as my final word, to make yourselves possessors of the virtue which God alone, through Jesus Christ, can give.

> " Who, O Lord, when life is o'er
> Shall to Heaven's blest mansions soar?
> Who, an ever welcome guest,
> In Thy holy place shall rest?
> He who shuns the sinner's road,
> Loving those who love their God,
> Who, with hope and faith unfeigned
> Treads the path by Thee ordained;
> He who trusts in Christ alone,
> Not in aught himself hath done;
> He, great God, shall be Thy care
> And Thy choicest blessings share."

THE RELATION OF RELIGION TO MORALITY.

Let us hear the conclusion of the whole matter; fear God and keep His commandments, for this is the whole duty of man; [or, as it is otherwise rendered, "for this is the duty of every man."]

ECCLESIASTES xii. 13.

THE author of Ecclesiastes seems to have given us a summary of the moral and religious speculations current in his day. With such changes of phraseology as the difference between Oriental and Occidental methods of thought and expression, and the products of modern science, may make necessary, the summary represents not inappropriately the speculations current in our own day. Certainly there are sentiments in the book crude and sceptical enough to satisfy the extremest free thinker of our time, but also there are sentiments reverent, devout, and true enough to be a perpetual joy to the Christian of every age. At one time the author says, "That which befalleth the sons of men befalleth beasts: as the one dieth, so dieth the other; yea, they have all one breath; so that a man hath no pre-eminence above a beast." In another place, he says, "Then I commended mirth, because a man hath no better thing under the sun than to eat, to drink, and to be merry." But the same author tells us again that as the dust returns to the earth as it was, so the spirit returns to God who gave it. Though he bursts forth in his address to the young man, "Rejoice, O young man, in thy youth; and let thy heart cheer thee in the days of thy youth, and walk in the ways of thine heart, and in the sight of thine eyes;" yet he adds, " but know thou, that for all these things, God will bring thee into judgment." And when he had surveyed the whole field of thought, he tells us, in the words of the text, " Let us hear the conclusion of the whole matter; fear God and keep His commandments; for this is the whole duty of man."

It is a twin thought which is presented, a two-fold proposition. It is an affirmation of what, during all time, has never ceased to be a subject of dispute, — the relation of religion to morality. The author affirms that they are indivisible. Expounders of Christian truth in every age, when they have expounded truth according to these utterances, have affirmed that religion and morality are ever indivisible parts of one whole; that a true religion is impossible without a true morality, and a true morality without a true religion. There is reason in our own day for a reaffirmation of the truth of the text; for not only have we, as a heritage of thought, all the sources of error which have prevailed in the past, but we have fresh discussions and seductive oppositions to the truth which belong especially to the present. In every age certain classes of minds have insisted that religion is itself the whole; have merged their morality in their religion; have made all to consist in worship, in raptures, in meditation, in devout thought. When reminded of the commandments of God, their answer has been, " He whose heart is busy in communing with God need give neither thought nor anxiety to the commandments of God." They have forgotten morality in the extremity of their devotion to religion. And this you will find not only among the Eremites, out of whom monasticism grew; not only among the mystics, — the metaphysical and the pantheistic mystics of the Middle Ages, — but in our own day it bursts forth in ever new forms, now in perfectionism, now in a boasted "inner life," now in some grand and unexpected discovery of an elevation toward which only the elect few can rise.

On the other hand stands another extreme which belongs to all time, which merges religion in morality, which insists that the sum of all requirements is found in a concentrated attention of the mind upon the particularized duties of life. They tell us it is not worship to which man is called, so much as to work; ever reminding us that he prays best who works best, ever thrusting before us the text of James, — which they misinterpret, — that "pure religion and undefiled before God and the Father is this, to visit the fatherless and widows in their affliction, and to keep himself unspotted from the world." Religion is lost sight of in the extreme attention paid to the minor duties of life. And in our times, new forms of opinion and speculation are directly tending toward a divorce of religion from morality. Thus every one who has observed the progress of Protestantism has noticed with something of alarm the extremes to which it has carried us. At the first, it grounded itself in the individualism of man. It rested upon the rights of conscience. It built itself solely upon individual convictions. It thrust aside priestly authority, and said to each man, " Stand up in thine own personality before God, and commune directly with Him whose child thou art." This, as a fundamental principle, has been carried in our day to the extreme of personal independence, at the expense, it might be said, of even Divine authority.

As a reaction from this extreme, we see on all hands, both among the extremely earnest and honest, and among varied classes who have no distinct philosophical reason for their change, a rapid movement from the extreme of Protestantism to the extreme of Churchism, to that which seems to afford refuge, stability, that which antedated Protestantism, that, under whatever name, which comes with the claim of authority from the Most High God, superseding the right of private judgment, of the individual conscience, and dictating to man what is requisite for commending himself to the Most High. Under varied forms, this has shown itself in different parts of our own country, — I may say over the whole civilized world. Nothing has been more apparent to the eyes of the observing than the rapidity of movement toward the restoration of mediæval practices, of mediæval forms of worship, of mediæval forms of thought. And just so far as men are taught to transfer the sense of personal obligation binding them to watchfulness and personal attention to the duties of life, just so far the danger is presenting itself of a divorce of religion from morality, of the old spirit and disposition unduly to exalt worship and to set it in the place of duty, in the place of stern activity.

A more recent and reactionary movement, again, is the philosophy of the Physicists, under whatever name presented; the philosophy of Evolution, regarding conscience itself as the product of human experience, moral laws as the deductions of human observation, everywhere setting forth the claim that morality is divisible from religion; that each human being, watchful of common effects, common sequences of action, may for himself discover personal obligations which bind him to his fellow beings, bind him evermore to a watchfulness of himself, to the subjugation of his passions, to the exercise of authority over his own spirit. So that it is maintained not only that morality is a possibility independent of religion, but that the true morality of our time must be founded in a philosophy divorced from religion.

Here, then, are two classes of teachers claiming attention, — the one unintentionally divorcing religion from morality, and the other doing so upon philosophical principles. It becomes, therefore, a necessity to ask, What is the true relation of morality and religion? Pray, what is religion other than our recognition of God and of our relation to Him? What are the religions of the earth but the collected phenomena representative of the inner convictions of the human heart in respect to the Invisible Power? What is morality but conformity to recognized obligations growing out of these inner convictions? What are moral acts but attempted fulfilments of moral laws written, first of all, on the heart? Can you separate the one from the other? As well separate the circumference from its centre; as well separate the vascular system from the heart; as well separate the nervous system from the brain to which it reports itself, and from which it receives its directive power. Religion is that which surrounds and controls and vivifies morality. It is that which teaches us our obligations to God and our obligations to one another. Morality is that which assures, convinces us of our obligations, because we are what we are.

But we must not forget that to the common apprehension there are grades, or degrees, of morality. We do not forget that morality is simply conformity to law, and that the man who obeys law is a " moral " man. But the degrees of difference between a morality which is the prompting of supreme selfishness, and the morality which springs from a recognized obligation to the Supreme Being, are removed by an almost immeasurable distance. Thus, in one respect, he is a moral man who commits no theft. Not to steal, is in that respect to be moral; not to commit any form of iniquity, is to be moral in respect to that kind of iniquity which is specified. So we might proceed to say that he is moral who is actuated solely by a fear of punishment; to go to a lower deep than that, we might say " He is moral indeed, though simply intent on gratifying the most selfish principle of his nature. He is moral who commits no theft, though he everywhere longs to possess what is not his own." But he who is moral for reasons above selfish ends, for reasons above the legal fear of a gratification of his baser instincts, is certainly possessed of a morality of a better kind; and ascending to that level which forgets the reward, forgets the penalty, which is ever intent upon the realization of the ideal being derived from the Archetypal Being, he is striving towards, and is rapidly acquiring, a morality of a vastly higher degree. So that when it is claimed that there are grades of morality without religion, it may not be denied; we grant that there are moral men who are not religious men. But we do affirm that the highest form of morality is impossible when separated from the highest form of religion; that a *true* morality is indivisible from a *true* religion.

While we say this, we do not forget the persistent claim which is put forth on all sides in behalf of a morality which is said to be practised for its own sake. Thus we never cease to be reminded that a morality is possible which is grounded in Atheism; that a morality is possible which is aimed at simply from a personal regard to morality itself. Pray, what is the meaning of this? What is an act which is performed for its own sake? What is that morality which a man is prompted to without a motive? When a man says that a moral act is performed for its own sake, if he means anything, he must mean that it is for the benefits which that act is certain to confer on him. The motive is found in that which accompanies the act. Or, suppose he says that by morality he means virtue, — means the personal good and the personal power to be moral. Why do we seek that? What mean we when we say we seek that for its own sake? We seek it either because of the advantage it gives us, or, for the peace it brings us, the happiness which accompanies it, — some quality inseparable from that which we call virtue, inseparable from the act which we call moral; that act is ever prompted by some beneficent result supposed to be connected with it. So that the boasted claim of a morality which is sought as its own end, is a morality which exists only as a mental fiction. It has no existence; it never did exist; it never can exist. There is no morality which is not accompanied by such qualities, such effects, such sequences, that he who is moral or virtuous expects in some sense to be benefited by them. Thus, when we speak of morality and religion, we speak not of two separate quantities, separate acts, separate modes of being, but of two sides of one great mode of existence. That man is religious who is truly moral, and that man is moral who is really religious. This will be seen, if we remember that the moral and religious nature of man are indivisible, that as component parts of man, they constitute one indivisible whole. Consider what is called the rational nature of man. To be a rational being is to possess the power to discriminate between objects. Reason itself is that power by which we distinguish between phenomena or qualities of phenomena. But he who is possessed of reason does not exercise it simply in distinguishing a straight line from a curved line, not simply in distinguishing between the proportions of figures, of dimension, of numbers; but he exercises it also in a discrimination of the difference between means and ends. And reason distinguishes not merely between the qualities of objects, but between the qualities of acts. So that to be a rational being is to be possessed of a power by which we discriminate between acts as good or bad. In other words, there exists no man possessed of reason who is not also possessed of conscience. Conscience is reason directed to the discrimination of acts, — discrimination between the qualities of acts. Any attempt, therefore, so to separate the rational from the moral as to make them independent parts of man, fails of necessity. For

I repeat that no man is so constituted that he distinguishes merely between things. He distinguishes between acts and between means as related to the ends sought in the acts. And not only is this true, but the moral nature which underlies the intellectual rests upon the religious nature; in other words, to be a moral being is to be a religious being. We cannot discriminate between acts, between laws binding on the human being, unless we also recognize the religious obligations which underlie his moral nature. This is seen even in the word. What is meant by obligation? What is meant by duty? Duty to what and to whom? Duty is not prudence. Obligation is not sagacity. When I look out into life as a man of business, when I look into society, and ask, with honest intention, how I can seek some indifferent end, I may exercise my reason only. But when I contemplate the relation of others, of society, to the end sought, my reason strikes down to the moral basis. And no man ever contemplates the right without feeling an instinctive desire to do the right. The obligation to obey the right is that which we distinguish as the quality of a religious being. The word religion signifies obligation; so that the terminology running through all morality belongs also to religion; the roots of all moral ideas are in the religious ideas of man. As phraseology belonging to ethics is essentially one with phraseology belonging to religion, so morality and religion are a unity, — indissoluble parts of one great whole in the spiritual nature of man.

But we proceed again to say that morality and religion are indivisible because morality needs religion to supply itself with adequate motives. We have said that a moral act without a motive is impossible. It is the motive which constitutes the morality itself when you come to analyze it. We have recognized a superficial morality, which men practise and account moral, independent of motives. Look over the face of society, everywhere observant of the proprieties of life. You say it is a moral state of society. Lift the veil and ask the motives. Your morality is dissipated. Go step by step onward, and ask, "What is true morality?" It is that which is founded on a true motive that will stand the test of analysis.

What, then, are the motives which morality regards? There are two classes of motives: one, where the motives ground themselves simply in the benefits conferred. This is utilitarianism, wherever you find it, under whatever guise, whether it be under the guise of religion, or under the guise of speculative philosophy. There is a vast amount of utilitarian philosophy under the guise of religion. That man who is moral simply from the fear of hell, has a kind of morality which is almost immoral when analyzed. That man who is moral merely from the desire of heaven, has only a microscopic amount of true morality.

Now morality dictated by utilitarian ends is morality which has its origin in the individual himself, and the plane to which it can raise him is never higher than the level from which it begins. I look out into the future of my life and ask, "Why shall I shape my course in a given direction?" and say to myself, "It is for the benefits I may derive." But these benefits are according to the dictates of my present perception of personal well-being. A utilitarian philosophy can never raise a man above the level on which it finds him. If men are raised in the mass, or as individuals, above the moral plane on which they began, it must be because the morality has some infused power, some infused life, some infused end higher than that which springs from human nature itself. Where do you find it aside from a true religion? Where do you find it aside from the Being who, opening His hands, scatters unnumbered blessings upon the race? Where do you find it aside from the Being who has opened His infinite heart and invited all to come and partake of His gracious bounty? Here there is a morality which calls the thought of the rational, moral being up to Him who is the Archetype of all. And that man who would construct to himself an ideal (as some of you, young gentlemen, have sought for that ideal in the year past), whence is he to derive it? The ideal man, the typical being ever to be set as an example,— where is he to be found? Can such an ideal be constructed out of the human heart? Is it a product of moral principles as deduced from observation? Is it other than that Archetypal idea which God Himself presents to us when He says to us, Be ye perfect even as your Father in Heaven is perfect? Do you find it elsewhere in the world except in the Person of Him who stood among us, the faultless Ideal, the perfect Man, the Divine-human Being, embodying in Himself the morality which He taught in precept?

Religion, then, we have seen, is inseparable from morality because of the inseparable union of the moral and the religious natures in man, grounded each on a common basis, and because there is no true morality — no true motive resulting in morality — aside from religion.

One other consideration: the necessity of religion in order to the production of that kind of character which morality is intended to produce. What is that? Morality is not for its own sake. Man is not required to be moral simply because morality will conduce to his present pleasure. Morality is for an end; moral law is a discipline. As well might you have said in these successive years of study, "The lesson given to us is for its own sake." There is either the luxury or the pain attendant upon the study of a difficult problem and the mastery of it. You have said, "It is for mental discipline; it is for evoking mental power; it is for training the whole being." Just so with moral law; it has an end. What is that end? It is to give you the power to stand erect; it is to give you character. Morality is worthless except it shall result in the rounding out of a complete and harmonious personality. How is this to be produced? Nothing is more simple and commonplace, whether in ethics or religion, than the statement that every man becomes like that object which occupies his supreme attention. That which is the object of your pursuit, whatever it may be, — if it is gain, if it is fame, if it is pleasure, — fame, gain, pleasure, each by reaction, produces a special type of character. So that the man whose thoughts revolve around a fortune has the characteristic stamp upon his very features; the man who is eager simply for the applause of men proclaims it in his eye, in the very step with which he walks among you. Look at him, from whatever point of view, you will see that all his thoughts are absorbed in commanding the homage of men. So he that presents before himself any other end, finds that the object in which his thoughts centre imparts to him its attributes. Where do you find the type of morality, the type of manhood, which you would make your end? Is it to be found among the great men of antiquity? Run your eye over the lengthened list, and select the man that you would put before you as your typical ideal. There is not one of all the hosts! Run your eye along the lengthened line of patriarchs, priests, prophets, evangelists. All imperfect! One, and One only, stands among men a Moral Ideal, — that Being in whom our religion was embodied, through whom God spoke, in whom God was manifest on earth. In Him is morality. And as your thoughts turn to Him, as your mind rests on Him, as you meditate upon His virtues and ponder His words, insensibly the attributes of His noble and ennobling nature pass to you, and you are elevated and translated and transformed into the image of God. This alone has produced among men true morality, — a morality after which men have evermore striven. Socrates strove for it, and boasted of the dæmon which the gods had granted to dwell in him, — a noble type, but not faultless.

So we fall back, not simply upon speculation, we come back to revelation; we come back to that which has been verified in the experience of the race, that which here in Jesus Christ is furnished to you; and when I say Jesus Christ, I mean religion, the true religion, the religion of God given to man. In that do you find the basis of a morality, — a basis immovable as the foundations of the throne of God.

Take, if you will, the type of character which the world has boasted of as the product of philosophy and not of religion, — the type of character presented to the rising generation as worthy of imitation, a type which is not, it is claimed, the product of a priestly religion, of the low standard of morality in the New Testament, but the product of a morality engendered by the spirit of modern science, fostered and built up into harmonious proportions, — what is the type of character thus presented? Beautiful, it may be, to behold in the distance, clear cut in outline, like the distant mountain as it stands against the horizon, snow-capped, serene, cold — not human. Take it at a nearer view, a morality chiselled, lifeless, as colorless as marble, as pulseless and wanting in human sympathies as the stone itself, — a morality that may claim to be touched by no stain of vice, but a morality wanting in the sweet sympathies of life; a morality that stands serene and elevated, but a morality that, like the glacier, recognizes the immutable barriers of law, and compresses and grinds itself slowly down towards the abyss, claiming to be faultless, but as wanting in sympathy as the soulless corpse. Which is the nobler type of morality, this, presented in our day aside from religion, unloving and unlovable, or that which is grounded in religion, which recognizes God as the Father of all, recognizes the brotherhood of man in his lowliest estate, recognizes the duty of sacrificing self, not for a name, not for fame, not for a brilliant discovery in science, but simply to bring back the wandering sons of God to a common Father. Which is the higher? Which is the nobler?

But there is another method by which the inseparable connection of morality and religion may be vindicated. *History* has established the truth that morality flourishes only as it is grounded in religion, and that religion is useful to man only as it coincides with and builds upon the immutable truths of morality.

In no age of the past do you find that a nation has prospered, that society has been stable, and all the fruits of good government have been manifest, unless the influence of a religious principle has been widely felt among the people. Just in proportion to the clearness and the stability of the religious convictions of the people, has been their progress and their safety. Just so soon as the religious convictions have become unsettled, just so soon the foundations of morality begin to decay, whether it be in ancient Rome, or in the later days of France, whether you go to the modern city of Calcutta, or into the narrow walks of the cities of our own land. Just in proportion as men have begun to lose their faith in God, their faith in the existing religion, just in that proportion have immoralities sprung up, vices become common, collapses of character become frightfully frequent. So that, looking abroad over our land, when the inquiry arises, Why are men high in religious positions making shipwreck of character? — the answer is, simply because they have divorced their religion from morality, because they have forgotten that God appeals to them individually, to their individual consciences, requiring them to be conformed to right, simply because right is founded in the eternal nature of God. When men come to suppose that morality has its origin in propriety, when they come to reason that moral obligations rest upon man only because of the established usages of society, then does society become unstable and the future uncertain; wrecks of character become frequent, and trusts are everywhere betrayed. But when morality is simply the product of immutable and implicit faith in God, then is character the resemblance, the reflection of that God in whom trust is reposed.

Young gentlemen, you have reached one distinctive stage in your career. It seems but a few years when your thoughts roamed as freely and idly as the air is now moving among the leaves of yonder trees. The future seemed to open out through a boundless vista; the very sunlight awoke you to activity. But the prison-house of life has been gathering slowly around you. The discipline of study, the discipline of thought, have brought you to serious reflection. And as you anticipate the future, the question comes to you, "On what am I to build? On what shall my character be reared?" You remember that moral law is enjoined upon you, addresses itself to you, not as a deduction from human observation, but that it proclaims to you what is wrought into the very constitution of your being; proclaims to you what is true of that Being in whose image you are made, and from whom you come forth. You have come to understand that duty is inexorable, that you can as soon escape from your own personal consciousness as escape from moral obligation. You have also come to understand that that Being who is invisible, everywhere present, speaks to you, not to the outward ear, but to the ear of the soul. God envelops you with His presence as the atmosphere does; your religious nature respires in the conscious presence of God, and your moral nature receives its activity, is invigorated by communion with that Being from whom all law emanated, from whom you have derived your being, in whom " you live, and move, and have your being," unto whom you must at the last return.

Let me remind each one of you here and now, that you will succeed in life just in proportion as you recognize your moral obligations to yourself, to your fellow-beings, and to God — to God, first of all; to man as the child of that God who is your Father; and to yourself as a being who, related to your fellow-beings, will be useful to others, and will be benefited by others, just in proportion to the control which you exercise over your own spirit. Build, therefore, each man, humbly, in the fear of God, under the Great Taskmaster's eye, because what you build, you build forever. It is not for a day, not for a year, not for a generation. As you sow, you reap. As you treasure up in your mind and heart, so will you travel endlessly with that acquisition, be it good or bad. You can never shake off what you receive in thought, in communing with yourself and with God. I charge you, therefore, as you go out into life, trust not to self, trust not to human guidance. There is one Being and One only, as I have said, to whom you can look. You need look to Him in no mystical sense. Look to Him not merely in the meeting-house, but look to Him in the market-place, look to Him when you stand at the bar pleading for the life of your fellow-being, or for his property, or reputation, better than life. Look to that Being when you stand by the bed of the sick, — that Being who alone can sustain the heart when it sinks and the strength when it fails; look to Him always and everywhere.

The Jesus Christ of the Bible is the Christ of humanity, not of the cloister, not of the priesthood; not the Christ whose benefits are to be conferred by a hierarchy. He is your Christ and my Christ; He is the Christ of all men. And I speak not as one who would set forth to you a religion distinct from morality. What one of you does not aspire to be moral? What one of you does not aspire to build up a character which God and men may look on with approval? What one of you would not say, " Give me a peaceful conscience, self-approval, though it be accompanied with poverty, persecution, and death?" You will have it when you look up serenely and say, " Keep me, O God!" and as you look into your heart and say, " Christ Jesus, the Saviour of men, the Guide of men, the Ruler of society, be Thou my Saviour." I commend, therefore, the Christ, in no narrow sense, as One who will put into your heart a hope which you may hide away. Rather, say that Christ — say it with an open face, say it by the wayside, say it in the mart, say it in the hall of legislation, say it at the bar, say it in the medical profession, say it wherever you are — say that Jesus Christ is that Being whom God sent to reconstruct society, sent into this world to teach men politics, teach men law, teach men all human duties; because He, and He alone, of all beings on this earth, represented in His own Person the perfect union of religion and morality.

I warn you, then, do not divorce your religion from morality. Do not go into the sanctuary on Sunday and chant your praises and say your empty prayers, and there leave your religion. Take it with you wheresoever you go. Build on it daily; never be ashamed, wherever or before whomsoever you are, to bow your knee as an humble worshipper, and say, " Father, God, keep me, " for this is your highest exaltation. Be truly religious, and you will be moral. Without religion, your morality will in the end prove a snare and a deception. God be with you, and Jesus Christ be in you, a Power to keep you, and the Hope of a glory to come.

INWARD UPRIGHTNESS.

As for me I will walk in mine integrity.
PSALMS xxvi., part of verse 11.

THESE are not the words of a self-righteous man; they are not the empty boast of one who had but a superficial knowledge of his own heart and its plague; they were the deliberate utterance of one whose unceasing prayer was, " Search me, O God, and try me, and see if there be any wicked way in me." It was the utterance of one who had known some of the bitterest trials to which man in this life is subject. His faith had been put to many a fiery test, and when he uttered these words, his own son, dishonoring the household of his father, had set himself deliberately to plot treason in the state. The heart of the nation wavered between the destinies of the son and of the father. Some of the father's most tried friends had proved wanting in this day of trial and extremity. The state was shaken to its centre; and as the Psalmist surveyed the desolation of his household and his nation, he fortified himself with the declaration with which the Psalm begins, " Judge me, O Lord, for I have walked in mine integrity." He narrates the perils that surround him, and exclaims, in the words which I have read as the text, " I will walk in mine integrity."

And you will distinguish here between the personal integrity of which he was conscious and the perfection of character to which the self-righteous man lays claim. The Psalmist says, not "I am faultless in my demeanor. I have been perfect and upright in all my course." On the other hand he says, in the Psalm immediately preceding this, and evidently written on the same occasion, "Pardon mine iniquity, for it is great." He acknowledged his transgression and his sins. He recognized the national calamities as the just consequences of his offences, and yet looking within, he says, "I have walked in mine integrity; and as for me, though my tried friends betray me, though mine own son lifts up his heel against me — as for me I will walk in mine integrity." It is possible for a man who is cognizant of defects in character to be distinctly conscious of an uprightness of purpose. It is possible for one who recognizes many a bald defect, many a deep, and almost incurable fault of personal character, yet to look calmly up into the face of heaven, and challenge the Divine scrutiny, to claim for himself rectitude of purpose, uprightness of spirit, fidelity of heart, unswerving loyalty to the Lord, who is supreme over all.

It is this conscious personal integrity that is the subject of our thought this afternoon, and the need of it, — its need in order to *personal character*, to completeness of character, to holiness of character, to a stable outward morality.

Inward integrity of purpose is requisite to outward conformity to the laws of God. Every man's character is the direct expression of his inward and ruling purpose. Character, whatever may be the influence of external circumstances, receives its determining force from the inner spirit. Every man *is* according to his *thought*. There is no such distinction, as we oftentimes hear, as that which is signified when we speak of "being" and "doing" as if the words were representative of different and distinct qualities. Every man *is* what he *does*; and every man *does* strictly in accordance to what in his inner being he *is*. And this outward expression of character will be complete and symmetrical, or defective and distorted, according to the simplicity or duplicity of the purpose within. He who is conscious of a single, pure, and upright purpose, sooner or later manifests that inward integrity to all men, and whosoever will, may read, and none can mistake. He who looks superficially even, but looks frequently, fails not in the end to determine the inward character. The outward is the expression of the inward. And in so saying we do not forget that external circumstances have their natural influence, — that birth and education affect naturally and necessarily the inward spirit. But the fixed inward purpose overcomes all that can be inherited, overcomes all that can be brought to bear from education. And still more, this interior purpose is dominant over all external circumstances. If it be true that the external forms the interior, if it be true that every man is simply what the circumstances of climate and soil have made him, as our modern philosophy teaches, then is it equally true that there is no such thing as a conscience in man — no such thing as a moral law according to which conscience controls the conduct of men. But as well might you say that the varying climates, as you ascend from the base to the summit of Ætna, which clothe its base with fields of green, with groves of orange and with teeming vineyards, which covers the middle course with deep and thickening forests, whose chill atmosphere crowns the summit with perpetual snow — as well might you say that these varying degrees of climate form the mountain and control it, as to affirm that the circumstances of a man determine the character of the man. As it is not the climate that forms the surface of Ætna, or that builds it up, or that sends forth the desolating lava, so it is not the external surroundings, nor climate, nor society, not inherited tendency nor physical peculiarities that make the man; but it is the inner thought, the ruling purpose, that which is conscious in the mind as the end and aim of life, that is stronger than all which is inherited, stronger than all that comes from without. It is the man's strength, linked with that of the Almighty, which makes him supreme. And this is the inward uprightness of which the Psalmist was conscious when he said: " I have walked in mine integrity," and " I will walk in mine integrity."

We do not forget that an external thought may fasten upon a man, just as the busy insect fastens upon the branch of a fruit-tree, bringing forth the excrescence which may destroy it. A thought fastening upon a man may shape and mould some of the constitutional peculiarities of mind and heart. But to do this it must be congenial with the inner and ruling purpose. No imagination can fasten itself upon the heart or upon the mind of a youth and draw him except it shall be in harmony with the inner spirit that rules him; and an evil thought which you in your impotence may say has been injected by your friend, is a thought which must become cherished, and must be in harmony with your ruling spirit, before it can shape and mould your character.

What is thus true of the character of the individual, is equally true of the character of the nation. So I mention to you as a second reason, the relation of this personal integrity to national character and institutions. The nation, from whatever point of view you contemplate it, differs in no essential particular from an individual. It is in a sense a person composed of many individualities; the type of national character takes its current and its shaping from the individualities that compose the nation. According, therefore, to the individual character and the individual purpose, will be the national type of character — will be also the national institutions. And the national institutions, so formed, manifest themselves again in the private walks of life. And in free governments the relation between the public institution and the more private life is very intimate. The relation between those who are known as leaders, or guides, or examples in society, and those who constitute the great mass of the national life is an inseparable one. That which rules the heart of the nation manifests itself in those whom accident of position or the careful training of education may exalt into places of distinction. They who are known in popular governments as leaders, as rulers, are at once the exponents of the public life and of the national ideas and spirit, and reciprocally, are the creators of these ideas and spirit. There is a close and inseparable correlation; they are at once the creatures and creators. The people find the reflection of themselves in their rulers; the rulers by reaction intensify and deepen the qualities of the ruled. So that he who would know the character of the national government may read it in those who are the recognized indicators of the popular life; and they who would know what is the national destiny or the spirit of a people may read it in the character of those who are its representative law-makers. Each is the counterpart of the other.

And in a nation where intellect comes prominently forward, defects in national life become all the more conspicuous and all the more dangerous. Educated men are, in a sense, representatives of the popular mind. The man who, in our day, enters upon a course of public education, gives hostages to the public that there shall be a right use of the knowledge he acquires and the mental discipline that he receives; he gives a pledge to the public that he will be an example to the mass. Why? He is supposed to have a wider, as well as a profounder view of life; he has ascended the hill of observation higher than the multitudes that are around him; he has looked more narrowly into the laws of his own being and the laws of the national life than his fellowmen. And more than all, he is supposed by virtue of his intelligence to be capable of self-control above the majority of his fellowmen. When, therefore, the people are misrepresented, there is naturally and inevitably a shock to the public sentiment. No matter what may be the position, he who betrays a trust, he who violates a moral obligation, he who turns the opportunities of official life to private gain, thereby wounds the public conscience. Doubtless there were other Chancellors prior to Lord Bacon who had been approached by clients who had business in the High Court of Chancery. But when the great Chancellor was known to have held out his smooth palm to receive successive bribes; when in the High Court of Judicature he had been proved guilty, and when in humble penitence and submission he acknowledged the indictment, the whole national life seemed for the instant to be arrested. The House of Lords professed to be, and doubtless were profoundly shocked. The whole nation raised its voice in indignation. Why? Simply because the heart of the nation had not been corrupted. There had been here and there individual instances of unfaithfulness. But when a great and marked example was manifest of one who had betrayed a sacred trust, one who had shown an inward want of moral integrity, then did not only the House of Lords, but the House of Commons and the whole nation justify the severity of the sentence, than which none was perhaps ever severer; only this could satisfy their deep sense of justice and uprightness and official honor. How much greater the condemnation in a free nation! Doubtless Benedict Arnold and Aaron Burr were not the only men into whose minds thoughts of treason in the early struggles and tumults of our country, entered. There is no evidence that any others ever cherished it, ever deliberated it. They did; and their names are synonyms for the profoundest infamy. They have sunk to a degradation from which no investigation, and no criticism, and no charity ever can raise them. Why? Simply because all over this broad continent there were individuals who said not only that they themselves would " walk in integrity," but who demanded that men who had been intrusted with places of responsibility should themselves be men of integrity. There is that wrought into the national life which no humiliation and no condonation of the crime can ever satisfy. Bear it in mind ever, — that there is that inwrought into the human soul which will not be pacified, which cannot be pacified, when men deliberately sell justice, allow themselves to be corrupted, and by their example seek to corrupt others. What is thus true of the nations in times past is true in our day. The heart of this great nation is not corrupt. The multitudes of the people are not deficient in personal integrity. And when any one in a high place of trust proves wanting, great as may be the pity, profound as may be the compassion, yet deep and ineradicable in every heart is the conviction that as a man sows so should he reap. He who has " treasured up thoughts of iniquity in his heart" must take his lot with the iniquitous, and go down to posterity stigmatized as a betrayer of trust, as one unfit to be recognized as a citizen of a great republic.

And thus we are led to another reason why this personal integrity is requisite. In the private and public weal, or happiness, is found a reason for it. What I have said thus far relates to the value of character to the individual and the demand for it in the nation. But there is also another and equally great necessity for it in the earnest yearning of all hearts for satisfaction, — satisfaction with self, satisfaction with the issues of life.

We may disguise it as we will, but there is after all a deep and settled yearning in all hearts for contentment, for peace, for happiness. And let us broadly distinguish between what is represented by these several synonyms and mere pleasure. He who seeks simply personal gratification in his daily life is certain to fail of it. He who makes his own personal gratification the sole end of his being, will be certain in each successive year to reckon upon what will result in an utter disappointment. No mortal can set that end before him with the assurance that he will ever reach it, any more than he who sets out deliberately any day of his life to say, "Now I will be happy to-day;" he will find before the day has closed that he has encountered one of the wretchedest of all the days of his being. Contentment, happiness, comes unbidden; but it comes as the inevitable sequence of an honest, earnest purpose to fulfil obligation. He who fixes his eye upon the stern requirements of law, law as he finds it in his own mind, law as he finds it asserted in his own conscience, will for a certainty find in each successive day a peace which no outward disappointment can arrest, a quietude which no external circumstance can disturb, simply because it is the natural result of that which is deepest in his own nature, his own constitution.

Look, if you will, at the closing years of the great philosopher and chancellor to whom I have referred. Did ever words more piteous come from human lips than fell from his? Out of the depths of that humiliation not only did he deprecate the royal wrath, not only did he seek to propitiate the nation, but deliberately did he write the bitterest of self-accusations, — the most unhappy of mortals, all the result of his own deliberate violation of this requirement, — the requirement of the inappeasable conscience, — integrity of life. Failing in that, he had lost all. In vain did men speak of the glory of his reputation, the greatness of the results to man, of the philosophy that he had propounded. In vain did men seek to calm the troubled spirit.

Look at another English statesman, one who, after a life of honest toil, at the close of his days, was smitten as few men in public life have been smitten. The hand of death snatched away a son on whom he had lavished a father's affections, in whom were centred a father's hopes and a father's pride. When Edmund Burke drew near the close of his life, and the men against whom, in the name of England, he had drawn the sword of justice, men against whom he had planted himself, and against whom, with his great eloquence, he had pleaded for justice, — when these men turned against him, when men in high places and low sought each to avenge his fancied wrong, the great statesman, in the unapproachable dignity of his self-conscious rectitude, could look out over the nation and look up into high heaven and utter words fit to be inscribed in letters of gold. These were the words of a man who had known what it was to serve, not self, but his sovereign and his God.

So might you find scattered along over the annals of the nation upright, heroic souls, who, suffering under calamity, deserted by friends, alone in the world, poor in this world's goods, were yet rich and at peace with themselves in the consciousness of having served God and the right. You will find them now in the private walks of life, and in the public places of the nation. They are men who have found in this conscious rectitude what no fortune can equal, what no reputation can offset, — men who, when they shall reach the conclusion of life, will not ask for the popular estimate, will not inquire what is the reward that the nation is about to bestow upon them, but who will look up into the serene heavens and say, " I have served my God, and I am content. I have sacrificed personal ends for the common weal, and I know that the reward is certain."

So also of national existence. There may be great national prosperity, there may be boundless gain, there may be victory over opposing nations, there may be what men account the supreme ascendancy among the nations of the earth. Yet there may be wanting this personal integrity of rulers and personal integrity of the private citizen. And I ask, *Are they a free people?* We in our great national struggle have overcome a gigantic wrong; we have torn up by the roots a long-planted and deep-seated national wrong and outrage upon our common humanity; we have erased it. We boast ourselves of being a free people, a great people. And yet are we free, except as we are possessors of this conscious rectitude of purpose, this uprightness of spirit? Are we free? There are various kinds of bondage. There is the bondage of the outward fetter; there is the bondage of the inward spirit; there is a bondage which comes from the love of gain, the love of pleasure. We may be assured that the national heart is not corrupted by any of the *external* circumstances of gain — of temptation. That which makes a people bondsmen is that which rules in their *hearts*.

> "There is a bondage worse, far worse, to bear
> Than his who breathes, by floor and roof and wall
> Pent in, a tyrant's solitary Thrall;
> 'T is his who walks abroad in the open air,
> One of a nation who within their hearts
> Must wear their fetters in their souls."

I will mention but one other reason for this need. It is found in the constitutional laws under which all men exist. What I have said thus far might be easily explained on the most common utilitarian principles. We might affirm that a nation should be upright simply for the advantages of good reputation, national prosperity, national happiness. There is something deeper than this. There are moral laws wrought into the very constitution of the moral being, so that it is not a matter of reward or penalty, but a matter of absolute and inevitable necessity of nature, that every man must live strictly according to the laws of his own being, that he who shall conform to these laws will find the inward peace that he seeks, and he who violates these laws will find that, by an inevitable necessity, the penalty is inwrought, is as inevitable as his own personal identity, and can be no more escaped than existence itself. To be is to be held by these laws. Now these moral laws belonging to every individual are equally operative in the state. So that whatever may be the external condition, whatever may be the surroundings of an individual or nation, whatever may be the general expectation or fear, certain it is that to do right is attended by its own inevitable consequences. To do wrong is equally followed by its own inevitable results. He then that will look within himself will find that these laws are part and parcel of his own being. You, young gentlemen, who have for the past years studied and looked into these principles, have found, like older and farther-seeing minds, that the moral laws which belong to the personal being, which are part and parcel of the personal existence, bring with them, by a slow but by the surest of all natural sequences, the good or evil which must result from your seeing and your choosing and your doing. Impossible is it that any man escape them.

But you will ask me, " Supposing what has thus been said to be true, what is the method of acquiring and retaining this conscious integrity? By what means can any individual become possessor of it? By what means can he retain possession of it?" These are practical questions. Varied and conflicting answers are presented in our time. The claim of no inconsiderable portion of the would-be public instructors of our day is that the moral teachings of the " popular religion," as it is called, have not been tributary to the public morality, as they should be. And it is declared to be one of the significant signs of our times that the highest teachers of physical science, that the accredited apostles of the new gospel, are models of character, examples for public guidance; that they are men who will not steal; that they are men who will not lie; that they are men who will not betray trusts. And the explanation of the claimed superiority of character which is presented is said to be that it is the natural product of the recognition of the inviolability of physical laws; whereas, we are told that the "popular religion" represents law as something variable, — law which is flexible, law which is enacted for special ends, and may be enforced or repealed according to the supposed will of the law-maker. This, it is asserted, is destructive of public morality. And if you recognize their explanation of the "popular religion" as just, the charge must be accepted as true; because nothing is more destructive of public morality than the supposed flexibility of law. A man who supposes that he may transgress to-day and to-morrow, and after a sufficient explanation or apology, be restored to fullness of fellowship with his fellowmen, be restored to a full birthright and the kingdom of God, who is taught that he may sin to-day and be righteous to-morrow, is a man who is directly decoyed into transgression. And if that be the preaching of our time, or the teaching of our religion, then it is pernicious. But is the charge a just one? Is this founded in truth? What is our religion? It does tell you that there is a possibility of escape from transgression. Physical science furnishes no escape. Physical science tells you that law — like the law of gravitation — moves unrelentingly, grinding into finest powder the man that encounters its action. Moral law also is invariable. It is inflexible; it is as immovable as the law of gravitation. God, the Almighty, cannot arrest it. He does not arrest it. But God, the Almighty, provides what physical science does not recognize or know. It is the possibility of recovery from transgression; it is the possibility of being reinstated. But the "popular religion" is not a religion which tells you that you can transgress to-day and be reinstated to-morrow, and transgress the day following and be reinstated at pleasure. It is not a religion that tells you that Christianity is a contrivance to cheat justice; that it is a contrivance to arrest penalty. On the other hand, where in the universe of God do you find a clearer enunciation of moral law, a more emphatic declaration of its inviolability, than you find in the teachings of this same Jesus Christ, whose religion has been denied? What says He? Why, "The heavens and the earth, which you Jews suppose to be immovable, shall pass away; the eternal hills, as you call them, shall be removed, but not one jot, not one tittle of the law can fail." Christianity is not a contrivance to show how to avoid law. It is a re-enactment of it; it is a reinforcement of it; it proclaims a hell eternal, and a heaven eternal. And while it so proclaims, it tells you that he who transgresses, though he be saved by Jesus Christ, bears with that Christ the irrevocable penalties of his violations of moral law. We do not escape; and it is only because an Almighty Being has descended and put His infinite shoulder under this great burden of human guilt that any one of us can awake with the consciousness of violated law, and in our sympathy with Him who died for us, fulfil that law. It is not abolished in any true sense; it is abolished only in a Jewish and external sense; it is re-enacted; it is written on the very heart; it is incorporated into the being; it becomes part and parcel of the person. Christianity, then, instead of being what certain teachers of the new gospel would tell us, — instead of being a contrivance to escape, — is a contrivance to fulfil. And this New Testament of ours teaches us that the design of it was to show how God might be just, — just in inflicting the utmost degree of penalty on every human being on His footstool, and yet justify the man renewed in Christ Jesus. God enforces law, — enforces it on you, enforces it on me. You never can escape it. It is wrought into the very fibre of your being, and you must bear its penalty here and hereafter; and in bearing it you will be enabled to escape only in that Being who, omnipotent, took upon Himself the burden of human guilt, and could say unto you and me, "Come unto me, all ye that labor and are heavy laden, and I will give you rest."

That is our Christianity; and if you ask how you shall obtain it, I reply that you will attain it, not by wrapping yourself in the conceit of your own intellectual strength and saying, "I see the law and I will conform to it." You see the law! You look up into the heavens and see the Supreme Majesty from whom all law emanates. Before Him you may say with the Psalmist, "Judge me, O God; try me; I have walked in mine integrity. But help me; pardon my iniquity, for it is great." This is Christianity, whether taught by David or by Paul. This was the Christianity of the early days of the Gospel, the Christianity of the Middle Ages; it is the Christianity of our own time. And if you ask me how you shall acquire it, I say to you, "Just as it was acquired of old." If you ask me how you shall preserve it, I reply, "Preserve it as it was preserved of old." It is not in man that walketh to direct his steps. The lot is cast into the lap, but the whole disposal thereof is from the Lord. What one of us, looking at himself and at his surroundings in society, can say, " I am equal to the day" ? What one of us, looking at himself with the Almighty, may not say, " God is on my side, and whom shall I fear?" With this conscious integrity, you may look up into the heavens and say, " God is my Father. I am reconciled to Him. Who is he that shall bring any accusation against me ? "

You will find it, then, as every man has found Christianity, not in private strength of intellect, not in self-conceit, but in humbleness of heart, leaning upon that God whose pity is over all, whose compassion fails not, who hears no cry that He does not answer, to whom no mortal lips utter a petition and there comes not back an answer of peace and rest.

Young Gentlemen of the Senior Class: The day that at the outset of your college life seemed so remote, has arrived. While you have been busily engaged in your pursuits, the hastening months have passed by, and the day which seemed so distant is now here. All the good and all the evil that you have learned in these four years is sealed up for eternity. As you have sown, so, God help you, you must reap. There are various days which form epochs in your career. None, perhaps, in your life, however long it may be, will be more marked than the day on which you close your college career. Other days may shed a more decisive influence upon your future course, but none will be looked back to with more of the feelings of gratification or regret, than the day in which you bid adieu to college.

Varied have been the lessons of these four years. Each year there came a voice from the unseen world that said to you, "Be ye also ready, for in such an hour as ye think not the Son of Man cometh." You had run only the first *stadium* of your course when Lincoln, who was abreast of the foremost of you as a scholar and as a Christian man, was snatched in an instant from the fulness of life to death. You had entered upon your second year, and Mathewson, sober-minded, earnest in purpose, grave in demeanor, the picture of health and strength, wearied and laid him down to die. In the midst of the busy thoughts of your Junior year, Ballou, wearying on a winter's day, turned aside to rest, and the Angel of Death called him from life. You entered upon your Senior year, — it was the last year of your course, — and Greene, inferior to no one of you in scholarship, noble in every trait of character, faithful in every relation, earnest in purpose, high in hope, turned aside from the course, and death took him. Four of your number in the four years have preceded you to the other world. These are solemn lessons for you to think of standing where you do to-day. Who of you during the next year shall bow his head and close his eyes upon the light of life? Young gentlemen, are you ready for it? What is life? What are all its hopes? What is scholarship, valuable as it is? What is anything you can set before you in life, compared with this inward *rectitude of purpose*, which I now, here in the presence of these spectators and of Almighty God, charge you to make yourselves possessors of. Take it into your hearts and say, looking up into high heaven, "God helping me, I never will dishonor the college that gave me my education. I never will dishonor the mother that bore me. In an age of corruption, in an age of recreancy, in an age of luxury, my first aim shall be *personal integrity.* With unstained hands, with an uncorrupted heart, with an unswerving faith, trusting in the power of Almighty God, and in the grace of Jesus Christ, I will stand firmly, I will quit myself like a man, I will be faithful unto the end."

And it is not inappropriate that I remind you of the words with which He who alone can keep you in life, ended His earthly mission, when, after a life of sorrows, He said, looking up to heaven, " I have finished the work Thou gavest me to do." Christ was then exalted. His Apostle, also, who followed in His footsteps, though it may be remotely, said, " I have fought a good fight, I have finished my course, I have kept the faith." Young gentlemen, can you name any end in life preferable to that, to be sought after? In the providence of God some of you may be called to places of high trust, — perhaps to administer justice; perhaps to plead at the bar of justice; perhaps to stand in the name of God as a teacher of religion; perhaps to be a teacher of the young. Wherever you are, I adjure you, be true to yourselves, true to your own consciences, true to that Christ who is able to help and save each one of you, to that God without whose blessing life at the best is wretchedness, is nothingness, is despair.

May the good providence of God protect you many years, keeping each of you by His mighty power, through faith, unto the salvation that is ready to be revealed.

NATURE AND CLAIMS OF MORAL LAW.

Who hast the form of knowledge and of truth in the law.
ROMANS ii., part of the 20th verse.

TO the ancient Jew, the law of Moses was declaratory of real and eternal truth. It contained no error, because it proceeded from an omniscient mind; it was founded upon immutable right, because dictated by a Being of infinite justice; it could not fail of being enforced, because it had been enacted by a Being of infinite power. It was sufficient to the Jew that it was the declared will of God. He asked no questions, but submitted as to absolute authority. But in process of time, the question arose, "Why the laws?" To devout men, the answer was sufficient, "It is the law of God." But the inquiry was still legitimate, "For what end?" Rational beings act from rational considerations, and the query was ever arising, "For what rational ends has God enacted moral law?" Later days and inquiries of the newest stamp rule out the question "Why?" as irrelevant and unanswerable. They tell us that law proceeds not from the will of an Infinite Law-giver, but from the personal nature of those to whom the laws are addressed. Moral laws, we are told by the latest teachers, are simply the accumulated experiences of the race; that law speaks not the mind of an Infinite and All-wise Being, not the mind of an Infinite Father, — God, — but the mind of the endlessly succeeding generations, — the father-man. So that law, they tell us, is not a transcript of the divine character, but of the human; law reveals what man is, they assure us, and not so much what God is, or what God determines. This is the teaching of science; and assuredly among all the results of modern science none stands out more conspicuously to the eye of the observing than the flood of light shed upon the moral teachings of the Bible. It was once sufficient to meet the moral declarations of the word of God by the assertion, " They are arbitrary; it is arbitrary and unjust in God to visit the iniquities of the fathers upon the children to the third and the fourth generation; unjust in God to sweep from the earth the iniquitous races to give place for better ones." Modern science dissipates all this by the law of heredity, which teaches us that hereditary evil is a first truth, and that the iniquities of the fathers are visited upon the children to the third and the fourth generations by the simple law of heredity, and not by the imposition of infinite power. We have now come to understand that laws are not forces impressed upon matter, as the horse is held in subjection, by the bit and bridle of the rider. Law is not something externally impressed; it is constituent in the thing that is ruled by it. Law is the most fundamental thought that belongs to any being or thing. You cannot tell why it is, but the root of all law is force; or, if you choose a better term, of energy; or, if still another, you may call it life. It is that indivisible, indestructible something that moves onward and moves by given modes. Its given modes you call laws, and by the word law you can express no more. The modes of matter are simply modes of force, — law's methods, according to which the force shall act. And what is true of matter, what is true of the plant which blossoms in your garden-bed, is true of the intelligent being that bends over the plant and admires the blossom. As the plant blossoms by its own inherent and constitutive principle, so the rational intelligence that cultivates it exists and moves according to its own constitutive, indestructible principle. We accept the declaration of science then when it tells us that law is not arbitrarily imposed of God.

Law is declarative of man's nature as well as of God's nature. It is declarative of man's nature because man was first himself declaratory of God's nature, — the old truth, not Biblical alone, belonging to all men and all philosophies, that man is the image of God. God is, and ever must be, the prototype of man. We are copies of Him. We accept, then, this modern teaching, if you may call it such, as not contradictory to God's word, but as confirmatory; we take those old, indestructible truths, brought up, if you insist upon it, out of Egypt, codified and speaking to you as they spoke to those who gathered round Moses for guidance, speaking to us all, real and eternal truth; we admit that these laws spoken by Him who spake as never man spake, illustrated in all these successive centuries, have been corroborated by modern science, and stand out to-day warranting an emphasis of the words of Paul to the Jew such as they never had before: "Who hast the form" (hast the expression, the representation, the real declaration) "of knowledge and of truth in the law." But when modern scientists tell us of their teaching, pray have they disproved the authority or the truth of the old law which says, first of all, "Thou shalt love the Lord thy God with all thy might, mind, and strength"? Is not the instinctive impulse to reverence as profound, as deep-seated, as indestructible in the nature of man as of old? Has science supplanted it? Take the other truth: "Thou shalt love thy neighbor as thyself." Has science improved upon it? Has it done more than confirm it? Take the whole round, — remembrance of the Sabbath, and all through the series. Is it less true to-day than of old, "Thou shalt not commit adultery"? Pray, has modern science disproved one of the moral teachings of Moses and of Christ? Have the sciences not corroborated, reiterated, reinforced, driven to the innermost soul of man, the conviction that the law is the form of eternal truth? Assuming this, what does moral law teach us? What are the lessons of moral law?

According to the teaching of science, law is representative of the nature of man. That is a thought I wish further to dwell upon. Granting that law is simply declarative of the nature of man, what does it teach us? First of all, *it teaches us the ground of the divine authority over us.* We meet the atheist here. We meet the modern scientist at the very threshold. We claim that according to his own teaching, moral law is constitutive of the moral nature of man. It teaches us what is the ground of the divine authority over us, but I might go back of that, and say that it first of all reveals God. It is not an empty earth that declares the divine Being?

You might wend your way over the trackless waste of a desolated earth, decked by no green thing, visited by no moving life, and you would see no evidence of God there. You would be like the blindfolded man, led amid the sounds of clanking machinery, who would hear the sighs and groans of some chained force, but would see no design. Unbandage his eyes and let him see the harmonious whole, working out some beautiful results, and there would be the thought that it had a maker. So in our world, clothed as it is with verdure, the physical subordinate to the vegetable, the vegetable subordinate to the animal, the animal subordinate to the intellectual, the intellectual subordinate to the moral, the whole ascending series, crowned not only by intelligence but by conscience, bespeak a personal Being, and no human intelligence can escape the thought; it is an irresistible conclusion, that where intelligence perceives a design, it must see a designer; wherever it takes up a result, it must see the author behind it. God speaks in it.

But then the ground of His authority, behind that, is because life, intelligence, is personal. You and I can look upon the forces of nature, confront them anywhere, and stand unmoved; men do it every day. The old prophet of Horeb fled to the cave on the mount, and sat down to his musings and repinings. The voice of God said to him, "Go forth." He went forth. The tornado swept by in its fury, levelling everything in its pathway; the earth upon which he stood trembled; the mountains toppled; all nature reeled around him, and he surveyed the scene and saw no God there. The thunder bolts dropped from heaven, smiting and melting whatever stood in their pathway. He saw no God there. But when "the still small voice" spoke, he heard God. There was no voice in the wind, no voice in the earthquake, no voice in the fire; but a still small voice spoke in the ear of his soul, and he wrapped his face in his mantle, and bowed his head. So is it of man everywhere. To be rational is to be conscious of some rational Being around us and behind us. You may go sounding your way out into the eternity to come; you may, by retrogression, traverse the eternity of the past, — you can find no stopping place where, as rational intelligences, you do not find yourself addressed by a rational Intelligence. It is because God is a Personal Being, that He has authority over us, my friends. We can stand before the impersonal authority of the state. Many a man has stood unblenched, facing all its associated, its combined terrors; but let a man nobler than you stand reprovingly as he looks into the depths of your soul, and you quail before him. You quail before him. It is not in your power to stand up and face the man. It may be a prophet looking into you and saying, "Thou art the man;" it may be the servant that trembles at your word. But wherever there is a man higher, or nobler, or purer than you, he is your master. It matters not what may be your kingly power, what may be behind your will, what may be your mere accidental trappings of wealth or elevation of position; all amount to nothing when a pure intelligence looks into the eyes of another intelligence and reproves it, and carries with the reproof the overwhelming conviction of right and of justice. So it is, then, in the presence of God. It is not because He is Almighty, my friends; it is because you stand alone with God, self-condemned. It needs not a voice to declare from the throne of God that you are guilty. Your own self-accusings overwhelm you in His divine presence, and that which gives to the authority of God its irresistibleness is that He is infinitely the best Being that looks upon this universe. The ground of His authority, then, is in the perfectibility of His own nature; the authority of God is original. We are made in His image. It is this principle of which I have been speaking, friends, that accounts for the apotheosis of the hero. How old Woden has sent his name down through the ages! How Thor, with his hammer, has been immortalized! All the calendars of saints, the apotheosis of men in polytheism, — hero-worship everywhere declares this truth. Man in his puny endeavors is ever seeking to put up something before him that he can feel worthy of his worship. It may be the Chinese bowing down before his ancestor; it may be the Romanist worshipping his calendar of saints; it may be the Christian philosopher rising up to the sublime conception of an Infinite Being, — but everywhere man has indestructible in him the instinct of worship. And this law declaring his own nature finds that there is an authority of God lying behind all power. It is in His personal nature.

There is a second lesson to be learned, — namely, *the inviolability of moral obligation;* or, to put it in other phrase, the inexorability of moral laws. If moral laws were simply the declaration of an infinitely wise being, then they might be as some shallow thinkers tell us they are. Law might be a flexible quantity that could be enforced or abrogated, according to the wise dictates of a ruler; a scarecrow that should stand up amidst the waste of human society to warn men, and which might be transfigured, transformed into an avenging angel, or might be torn away, or banished, after accomplishing good to society. Is moral law such a thing? Has it simply been devised for the end of society, or shall we believe, rather, as does the modern scientist, that law is as indestructible as personal identity? It is that which constitutes identity. It is that which makes man the man, and distinguishes him from the brute; that which constitutes all that is distinctively peculiar to man is the moral law upon which he is organized. If this be so, then you will at once see that it is not within the power of fiat, it is not within the possibility of power, even omniscient power, to abrogate law, to arbitrarily wipe away the penal consequences of violated law. Law can no more be arrested by fiat, no more abrogated by decree, no more taken away by any external contrivance, than you can take away the identity of the personal being which is constituted by it. And if such be the moral law, then you will readily see the significancy of the primitive power of conscience. That which makes the terrific power of conscience is that it is the individual judging himself. It is man simply confronting himself and judging himself. Were it another external being, we might appease him. But can man appease himself? Can he change himself? That which makes the terror of it is, that he is both judge and culprit. He is himself the source of the law, and the source of the judgment pronounced according to law. So that when

Milton tells the story of Satan's terrific exclamation, there is truth in it:—

> "Me miserable! Which way shall I fly
> Infinite wrath, and infinite despair?
> Which way I fly is hell; myself am hell;
> And, in the lowest deep, a lower deep,
> Still threat'ning to devour me, opens wide,
> To which the hell I suffer seems a heaven."

This is profound truth, friends. That which constitutes the terribleness of moral law, that which gives the implacability to conscience, is that man is the being judging himself, and judging himself according to the immutable laws of his own nature. And when we so look at it, we understand again the words of Job:—

"In thoughts from the visions of the night, when deep sleep falleth on men, fear came upon me, and trembling, which made all my bones to shake. Then a spirit passed before my face; the hair of my flesh stood up. It stood still, but I could not discern the form thereof. An image was before mine eyes, there was silence, and I heard a voice, saying, Shall mortal man be more just than God? Shall a man be more pure than his Maker?"

If I condemn myself, as we have said, shall I be more just than God? If I flee in terror, shall I not, as I look up into the presence of the Eternal God, see the same calm, unbroken stillness saying, it is just? Law is inexorable, and, my friends, you never can escape the penal consequences of wrongdoing any more than you can escape yourself.

Take the wings of the morning; fly to the uttermost

parts of the earth; descend to the depths of hell; climb the battlements of heaven; go where you will; so long as you are with *yourself*, you will find that moral law cannot be trifled with; that it is inexorable, immutable, infallible as your own personality is indestructible.

Again, there is another lesson to be learned from this, — *the ground of personal rights and their sacredness.* Very general attention has been concentrated in our day on the ground of human rights. These rights have a two-fold aspect, — rights in their relation to God, and rights in their relation to our fellowmen. These two cover the whole ground of human rights. It has been asserted by a class of writers, and by one, indeed, a Scotch writer of our own day, a man who has not yet reached middle age, with some degree of force, that man has no rights in relation to God. He scorns with lofty indignation the theory of Pessimism. He is roused up into a sort of moral, lofty objuration against the idea that God could predestinate man " to damnation." And yet he tells us that " man has no rights in relation to God." And the sole ground of his assumption is that personal existence is the gift of God, and that the mode of the existence is determined by the will of God, and that if God does thus originate life, He has the right to control and direct it. The reasoning is false. We may say it reverently, say it here in the divine presence, but say it calmly and distinctly: If God makes me a rational being, He has endowed me with inalienable rights in my relation to Him, under His government; rights which He can no more invade than He can overthrow His throne, and rights which we may say, and say devoutly, God Himself bows before with infinite respect. My friend, God may not invade one of the rights of your personal being, to save you — not to save you from eternal death. He works not arbitrarily. He works in accordance with law; and He, having made you a personal being, capable of choice, has put within your power the determination of what you will be in the future. It is not *imposed* upon you. But, by virtue of having constituted you a free, voluntary being, He has endowed you with the right to exercise your volition. You *do* exercise it. God will not interpose or interrupt its exercise. This, we think, is an answer to the declaration that " we have no rights in relation to God."

But there are rights in relation to man; and how have men prated endlessly in their defence. Rivers of blood, through century after century, have flowed simply in their defence. Nations risen to glory, possessed of wealth, intelligence, have dashed themselves one against the other, scattering the earth with fragments of their ruin, all in defence of imaginary rights. Forever are our ears dinned with the declaration of " our rights." Our own national existence began in a defence of them. Great Britain declared that it had a right to tax its American colonies, " to shear its American wolf " (as the opponent of the system called it), and the American colonies declared that they had a right to shear themselves, and in maintenance of that right they were ready to lay down life. What constitutes " the sacredness of our rights"? Why is it that nations and whole generations have been ready to surrender their existence rather than forfeit their rights? Why? What are the foundations of my rights? Simply, "That I am a personal being?" No, my friend, but the profoundest ground of my rights lies *in my obligations.* I have no rights if I have no obligations. I cannot plead a right to life, a right to liberty, a right to the pursuit of happiness, a right to property, except upon that ground. All these depend upon my duty.

First of all are laws that bind me to God. This is the question which has arisen in every age, "Judge ye whether it be right to serve God or man," — *i. e.*, whether it be right to follow my moral convictions, obey the laws of my moral being, though thus I allow myself to be plundered, robbed, enslaved. I have no rights except just so far as they are requisite to the fulfilment of my obligations. What is the ground of my right to take another man's life, rather than have my own sacrificed? Simply the obligations laid upon me. I am a citizen, I am a father. There are those looking to me, there may be those dependent upon me. I have no right to allow myself to be lawlessly sacrificed, because I have obligations. Behind my rights everywhere will be found stern, implacable, inevitable, inexorable laws. And it is because there are moral laws that bind me to God that I am not at liberty to allow any man to interfere with the fulfilment of those laws. It is because I have laws binding me to my fellow-creatures that I have no right to allow the assassin or robber to plunder me; by plundering me he disables me for the performance of my moral obligations. If I have no obligations, if I vacate laws, my rights are gone with them.

Every man recognizes this when he talks of human

slavery. Every man recognizes this when he goes thoroughly into an analysis of what constitutes "right." So that in our day, when men tell us that moral rights spring simply from "personal being," we deny it; and we say to every man: "First of all, fulfil your obligations, and then prate about your rights." Underneath all rights are the duties which you owe to God, to yourself, and to society. Fulfil these, and in fulfilling them you will maintain "your rights;" for in all cases rights accompany the fulfilment of moral obligations.

There is another lesson learned from this. It sets before us *the highest aim of man in life.* Let us recapitulate. We have said: The theory that moral law reveals the moral nature of man, first teaches us the ground of the divine authority over us; then, secondly, the inevitability of our moral obligations, or the inexorableness of the laws of our moral being; and, thirdly, the ground of our moral rights and their sacredness. Our next thought is: The true destination of man, or the highest aim which a man can set before him. What is it? Why, manifestly a complete fulfilment of all the laws of his moral nature. There is no higher aim, because, in fulfilling this aim, the fulfilment of every other necessarily follows. I am not unaware that it may be asserted that this is a selfish view of man; that he who fixes his eye solely upon himself, asking if he is fulfilling the laws of his being, isolates himself from society. This is a mistake, friends. As you and I came down the sidewalk to-day, we stepped carefully. Masses of stone had been thrown up from the level. Why? The little rootlets, so feeble apparently, in obedience to the energy that was in them, seeking to fulfil their mission, searching for nutriment to send up to the giant tree above, put forth a force which lifted the mighty pressure that had been put upon them, threw it up from the level, asserted its inherent strength. Chain the force wherever you will, it affirms its " right." So there are laws, — laws of your nature. First of all is that instinctive necessity of looking out for and finding somewhere a support. The young vine that shoots up to-day, soon to be loaded with clusters, stretches out its tendrils for support somewhere, — support against the rude blast that will soon come. What are you and I, with all our glory and all our power, but feeble tendrils, seeking, groping, somewhere, for something to lay hold of that will keep us steady in the commotions and turmoils of life? Where is it? Shall I trust in man whose breath is in his nostrils? Shall I trust in man? He will deceive me. In the very hour in which I shall depend on him he will be gone. No; there is that within you, my friend, there is that in every one of us, reason about it as you will, which forces you to look outward and inward for something to cling to, which forces you to say, " Oh! where is that which I can lay hold of and feel secure?" God is that only support. So I say, that to fulfil this law of your being is not " selfishness."

You belong to society also. You cannot escape society. If you flee from man, you still sigh for man. It is only a desperate remedy for a diseased intellect that leads men to seek solitude. The normal condition of man is association, society, friendship, love. You crave it; you are solitary and helpless without it. To fulfil the law of your being is, then, to fulfil your obligations to your fellowmen; you cannot love yourself properly and not love your fellowmen; you cannot love your fellowmen and not love yourself; so that this love is not "selfish." The grandest philanthropists that tread the earth are men that feel stirring within them the impulses of the indestructible laws of their being, which bind them to God and bind them to their fellowmen, and they realize their own highest ideal just in proportion as they realize their relation to God and to their fellowmen.

What were this earth without that energizing power that comes from the blazing glory above us, that dazzles us as we gaze at it? Blot it out and you blot out all life from the earth. Blot out God from human thought, blot out the idea of God from human society, and you bring only desolation and emptiness. Take man from his relation to his fellowmen, and you have made society a blank, you have turned the race to destruction, you have unpeopled the earth.

So all the obligations that belong to us will be fulfilled just in proportion as man asks earnestly and patiently, "How shall I fulfil these laws of my being?" He loves God best who loves all men best. He loves all men best who is most profoundly, self-respectfully intent upon fulfilling the laws of his nature. So that he who realizes this ideal of himself most perfectly is one who is the son of God and the son of man.

You may ask me, "Is this all?" I have presented before you a picture which is severe, — laws, grinding laws, laws everywhere. The moral order of the universe must be maintained at every hazard; physical order is subordinate to moral order; it must prevail. Is that all? Then certainly life were a saddening spectacle. Generations hastening across the face of the earth, burying their dead, wiping their eyes, hastily turning away and asking, "Oh! is there nothing but this?"

God rent the veil. The Son of Man came. The Son of Man, who incorporated all these laws, so that when He spoke moral law, He spoke it intuitively. He did not arrive at it by induction; He did not arrive at it by deduction. He spoke it because He *incorporated* it; He lived it; He *was* the moral law, speaking out to the race. And He not only fulfilled it, but He made it possible for you and me to fulfil it.

Christ uttered no weightier truth in all His teachings than this: "Think not that I am come to destroy the law or the prophets, I am not come to destroy, but to fulfil." Christianity for its first, its last aim, sets before you and me "the fulfilment of the law." Be assured, my friends, Christianity is not a contrivance to evade law. It is not a scheme that is intent only upon arresting the penalty of law. It does "arrest penalty," but it arrests it for the one sole reason that Christ may be formed in us, and we may through Him be conformed to law, — *conformed to law*, not *released* from it. It is rewritten in us. It is made to shine forth in Him as it never shone forth before. And the Christian man, instead of finding morality separated from religion, instead of finding religion to be a scheme or device, "how not to do it," finds that its one single aim is "how to do it." And there is nothing that is so intently called for in our time as the preaching of the Gospel as the scheme of God to fulfil law, fulfil it in the counting-room, fulfil it in fiduciary trusts and positions, fulfil it everywhere. And Christ stands up bearing the penalty and saying, "Whosoever will, let him come unto me;" for the express purpose of bearing that penalty for you, and re-writing that law in your heart, He is at once the Son of God and the Son of Man.

Therefore, when the scientist turns to us and says, "We accept the philosophy of your religion, but not the facts; we accept the spirit of your Christianity, but not Biblical teachings." We reply, "Friend, they stand or fall together." We accept the declaration of science, then, when it comes to us, with its theory of life, showing that every moral teaching of the Bible is as immutable as God's throne. But, further, we declare to you that Christ stands immovable. You can no more displace Him from history than you can displace moral law. You can no more blot out of literature the moral teachings of Christ than you can blot out from the heavens the sun. Christ exists for all time.

Gentlemen of the Graduating Class: The truths to which your attention has been invited rest upon a foundation with which you are not unfamiliar. These truths are the application of principles to which for a few months past you have been directing your special attention. I shall rejoice if there has been wrought into your mental constitution the ineradicable conviction that the first aim of life is the fulfilment of duty. The question, "What is duty?" is not the watchword of our times.

In this day, the watchword is, "What will pay?" As you look out into the future, gilded visions allure you. Pathways stretching o'er hill and dale invite your steps. You will meet tempters by the way. There is but one safeguard. Carry with you always, as a controlling, an ever-present thought, "What does God require? What is the requirement of that moral nature which I am to carry with me through life and into eternity?" Wealth, as you may acquire it, may take wings to itself and vanish. Reputation is but a breath. The applause of men will not soothe the gnawings of a guilty conscience in your closing hour. Let me assure you that no truth stands more absolutely demonstrated in history than the truth that as you sow you must reap. Sow truth! Never violate your consciences under any pretence. And as you look out into life, remember that there is One who will follow you, — One to whom your moral nature will respond; and there is no place in the universe of God in which you can hide from His searching; and there is no place in the universe of God in which He will not beam gladness into your soul, if, with honesty and humbleness of spirit, you hold fast to righteousness and truth. The end will come. It may come very soon to some of you. No man knoweth to which one of your number the "star" upon the printed catalogue shall first be affixed. God knoweth. Some few of you will travel out over that long, out-stretching pathway to which I have alluded. Not he who lives longest has the most to be thankful for. He who lives most faithfully is the one that has the most honest ground of rejoicing before man and before God, — before that

Lord and Saviour of whom I have spoken, to whose teaching let me commend you, whose religion I warn you now, in this presence of the Most High, not to forget and not to deride, not to speak disrespectfully of, not to neglect. For, when you come to the hour of death, what can console you but the presence of that merciful Being who created you, and provided for your happiness in this life and through eternity? I have spoken of the Lord, who is the Teacher and Saviour of men. He passed away from earth long before the period at which men ordinarily are called to withdraw. And you remember His words, while the impenetrable cloud of darkness was resting upon His spirit; He lifted up His eyes to God — it was a moment of rejoicing such as the record of His life nowhere else furnishes, when He said: "I have finished the work Thou gavest me to do." By God's help, finish your work manfully, in the spirit of Christ, and Christ Himself will receive you, that where He is, you may be also.

THE SENSE OF DUTY.

O that my ways were directed to keep Thy statutes!
Psalms cxix. 5.

INNUMERABLE as are the objects of human pursuit, the motives which prompt us to pursue them are relatively few, and all centre in personal beings. Motives, and especially moral motives, never terminate in mere things. The artist paints his picture or chisels his statue for the gratification of his own taste, or of the taste of some other personal beings. And if our motives ever appear to terminate in things, it will be found that they are such things only, as are in some way brought within the great kinship of life. We may pity the brute; seek to rescue it from its sufferings, to save it from famishing, — but because it possesses life. We may look tenderly, even compassionately, upon the drooping plant, and seek to restore it; but it is because the plant comes within the kinship of life. Motives springing from personal wants are various, and if left to their own spontaneity are liable to mislead. The whole family of personal beings are bound together by great moral laws, — laws from which none of them can escape with impunity. It is the design of moral laws to regulate human motives. Unregulated motives lead to irregular conduct, to distorted characters; distorted characters to the disruption of society; disruption of society to moral anarchy; and moral anarchy to extinction of human hopes and the despair of mankind. Every intelligence open to the discernment of moral laws will be prompted at times to exclaim in the language of the Psalmist, in the text, "O that my ways were directed to keep Thy statutes!"

The sense of duty in human action is a theme of vast proportion. It is one that presents itself to us in our day, under increasing light, and speaks to us with unwonted emphasis. Let us inquire why we all, especially those of us who are starting out upon the great career of life, should seek to comply with this sense of duty.

The sense of duty should rule us because, first of all, it is unappeasable except by obedience to it. It springs into the human breast from the discernment of our relation to the right. To see the right clearly is to be immediately conscious of the sense of obligation. The sense of duty, therefore, is as ineradicable as is moral law. The great laws of this universe are not imposed upon matter, — not, as popularly represented, impressed on it. Physical laws are not great chains to hold inanimate matter in organized form. They are in the very atoms of which matter is composed. Physical laws are in the very constitution of the material universe. Where matter is, there are laws. And equally true is it that where human beings are, there are moral laws,— moral laws, not impressed on them, not prescribed, but in the very constitution of the personal being, as much so as are the great physical laws that hold the boundless complexities of systems in our universe in harmony and order. So moral law, by the very constitution of personal beings, holds them with a relentless grasp, and duty cannot be escaped. We may fly from it to-day; to-morrow it confronts us. We may take the wings of thought and flee to the uttermost parts of the earth, and seat ourselves, as we think, in security; but suddenly and imperceptibly it comes face to face with us and exclaims, "Lo, I am here." "Canst thou bind the sweet influences of Pleiades or loose the bands of Orion?" Canst thou by analysis resolve the constitution of man and dissipate moral law? If thou canst, then thou canst prescribe some way by which poor mortals can flee from duty and seat themselves apart from it. It is inevitable, and its voice cannot be hushed except by patient and faithful compliance with its demands.

But duty is not alone the voice of law. Duty is the "stern daughter of the voice of God." There are those who tell us that duty is a fiction of the mind; it is the calculation of prudence; it is a spectre which the human mind in its thinking finds cast before it. As the traveller, standing upon the Bröcken heights in the Hartz Mountains, finds his own stature drawn out in gigantic outlines; sees the spectre image before him, so they tell us, the thought of God is but the image of man projected into the blank spaces that are before him. That which we call the voice of God, they tell us, is only the echo of man in his helplessness and wailing thrown back in derision upon him from the emptiness of space above him, —

"Heaven's roof to them
Is but a painted ceiling hung with lamps,
No more, to light them to their purposes."

Is there ever a spectre without a spirit? Is there ever a shadow without a substance and a light to fall upon it? Are these thoughts written all over this earth, packed into the very rocks, piled up into the very heavens, and is there no thinker? Are we the only deities? If there be minds to read thoughts and to trace footsteps, then there has been a thinker to write the thoughts; there has been a step, — the step of Deity to mark the plains of earth. The voice we hear says to us not "this is better," "this is wiser," "this is prudent," and "that is unwise, imprudent;" but it says with all the imperativeness of almightiness and infinite wisdom, "Thou shalt." When I hear within me the voice, "I ought," I also hear, "I must." Duty is the voice of God. But we may be told men have mistaken the voice. There have been great and good men who thought they were obeying the voice of duty, and they were deceived. It was the voice of the arch deceiver. Did not Paul in the sincerity of his heart persecute the Church of God, and think most devoutly that he was fulfilling the highest obligation? Did not, they ask us, Calvin give his sanction to the burning of Servetus? Did not John Knox, in the ardor of his heart, counsel the execution of Mary, Queen of Scots? Did he not counsel the slaughter of her counsellors and supporters? Have not great and good men continually been mistaken? Yes, doubtless; but never did a good man and earnest man, seek honestly to know his duty, but, in due process of time, he found it; and though he may have mistaken it, he mistook it only amid the boundless confusion and power of human error that surrounded him.

We should also obey the dictates of duty because of its relation to our personal happiness, — the lowest of motives, it may be; but as much as for life, we yearn for happiness. God makes the love of life and the love of happiness to be the test and measure of our duty to our fellow-beings. To love our fellowmen as we love ourselves, to seek their happiness as we seek our own, are human duties; to seek happiness, therefore, is not only an instinct, but a duty of the human spirit. How shall we find it? The happiest men are not those who follow the fickle guidance of appetite or fashion. The most wretched of beings, that sit down to moan, to write bitter things against themselves, are those who find standing all around them the frowning duties of life neglected, or spurned. There is no blight, no mildew, that can fall upon the human spirit, so certain to blacken it, no shadow so certain to ruin it for this life and the next, as that of a neglected duty. What we call human penalties and human rewards, when we come to analyze them, are nothing more nor less than the natural action of this sense of duty. Complied with, it fills the soul with sunlight and joy; what men in their own language call heaven. That heaven about which so many unthinking men prate — what is it, after all, but the clear, serene atmosphere into which one ascends, carrying with him the consciousness that he has done his duties faithfully; that he has fought the good fight? What is that blank, dark, dank prison of hell but the accusing voices of neglected duties? What is it, after all, but the gnawing sense that "I might have done it, and I failed to do it;" "I ought to have done it, and I left it undone"? So all the way through life, the man whose countenance is haggard, whose spirit is unresting, whose soul is burdened, whose step is unsteady, is the man who is ever pursued by this sense of unfulfilled obligations. And the man who looks, though it may be with saddened features, yet with serene aspect, into the events of his life, or, the man whose step is merrily elastic, is the man who carries the clear consciousness within himself that he has done according to the measure of his ability, has sought diligently and daily to do his duty as God has assigned it to him.

Further, the faithful performance of duty stands in an unalterable relation to character. Character may be looked upon in two lights. The human soul may be conceived of as a simple essence capable of illimitable expansion, susceptible to every variety of impression, and character as the result of the impression which the surrounding duties of life leave upon the soul. As you all know, the word in the original Greek meant simply the stamp, the die; then the impress which the stamp leaves upon the yielding substance. So, character is simply the resultant, the stamp left by the fulfilled obligations of life. He who flees from them, fails of that symmetry of development, that harmonious proportion of parts which would come from standing firmly amid the pressing duties of life. He who holds himself with unflinching and unwincing purpose, steadily up to the stern duties of life, finds that they leave a permanent impress upon him, and this impress we call his character.

You may conceive of character in another light. The human spirit may be regarded as a combination of subtile forces, — too subtile to be ascertained by analysis; forces of instinct, of appetite, of imagination, of reason, and will; all co-existing, each liable to show itself independently of the others; each intended to be so wrought in with the others, so to be knit together with all the others, so to be braided in and held, as that man shall be complete, organized, and, with all these forces maintained in their proper strength and relations, that he shall be possessed of what we call integrity. This is character under another aspect, and it is alone obedience to the sense of duty that gives it.

There are men, the threads of whose moral life are flying all abroad, who show to you that they are incomplete, disorganized, incapable, destined to confusion, overthrow, and ruin. They are not men possessed of character; and character, I may here add, is closely akin to reputation. Men, in the long run, never fail to judge aright their fellows. Every man in this great battle of life is sure, sooner or later, to obtain, in the estimate of his fellowmen, his just deserts. There is an eternal justice in the processes of the eternal God, by which every man will, unerringly, receive his own; and the reputation, which men so much prize, rests only in the end on solidity of character.

There is another reason why we should give close, unremitted attention to duty. It is found in the prevailing conceptions of popular Christianity. Every age has its own types of Christian thought, and consequently its own types of character, — types of thought that impress themselves upon society, and produce its types of character. The type of Christianity prevailing in our own day is worthy of the most devout and careful attention of every man. The tendency everywhere is to make Christianity simple, easy of possession, — as if, one might almost say, a universal strife exists among the sects to see how easy they may make it for men to enter into the kingdom of God; and the people long to have it so, — rejoice in being told that Christianity can be taught them in six short and easy lessons. It is so much easier to burn incense, to do obeisance to empty names, to bow before imaginary deities on human altars; so much easier to cultivate fervid emotions by the singing of doggerel rhymes; so much easier to tithe mint and anise and cummin, than to sustain the weightier matters of the law, — that the people love to be told that a paroxysm of pain succeeded by a paroyxsm of delight is the whole work of Christianity done once for all. They delight to be told that all is completed when a man is born into the kingdom of God, — as if the whole work of Christianity merely amounted to the declaration that they are disciples of Christ. Christianity reconstructs personal characters, and reconstructs society, and the religion of Jesus Christ is a religion of law. Christianity is not a device to evade law, to blot out the penalty of law, but, on the contrary, it is the re-publication, the enforcement of law.

When we look at this popular tendency, need we be surprised at the results? Religion doubtless never spread itself so widely over society, or struck so deep into the heart of society, as it is doing to-day. And yet, why this general breakdown in public morals? Why these betrayals of trust? Why these briberies at the bar, and in the halls of legislation? Why this moral cowardice in the pulpit? Why the narrow bigotry? Why a conception of Christianity which is founded upon some fragment of doctrine, rather than that comprehensive view that takes in the whole horizon of thought, — that charity which is serene and transparent and comprehensive as the atmosphere that surrounds the globe? The religion of the Lord Jesus Christ is a religion that teaches us that first of all is law, last of all is law, — law at the beginning, law in the progress, law in the consummation.

And there is another consideration. The design of Christianity is simply to bring law, or sense of duty, and love, or spontaneity of soul, into oneness. The aim of Christianity, I say, is to bring man to that condition where he shall love law; where he shall say, in the language of the Psalmist, "O how love I Thy law! It is my meditation day and night." Observe, if you will, how the great Founder of our religion began His career, simply by teaching law. How He declared with emphasis the word which I have already read, "Think not that I am come to destroy the law and the prophets. I am not come to destroy, but to fulfil." That was His first lesson. He illustrated it in all His life. He embodied that law in His personality; He looked it out of His eyes. It spoke from His lips. It radiated from every feature. And He said to His disciples, "Unless your righteousness shall exceed that of the Scribes and the Pharisees, ye shall in no case enter into the kingdom of God." From the beginning to the end, He reiterated moral law; and more than that, in His example, when occasion came, there was no evasion; there was no narrowness; there was no pleading for excuse or release; and though his soul was crushed with agony such as no man ever may comprehend, he said, " Nevertheless, not my will but thine be done."

Who are they, then, that tell us that Christianity is perverted? that Christianity is a religion of freedom — not a religion of duty? In the name of my Master, in the name of that holy religion which He founded, I protest that Jesus Christ taught in His example that the first thought of the human spirit should be, " What is my duty?" When they tell us that law historically preceded Christianity, and therefore has been abrogated, they misunderstand it. Law was not historically before Christianity. Christianity was older than law. Law simply presented to mankind one aspect of the Christian religion. Christianity was older than the law. Christianity to-day, when it comes with its announcement to man, comes with its unalterable command, ye shall do the will of God, or perish. That is the religion of Christ to-day.

Nor did Christ only yield to duty, but His servants also. Hear those servants when they speak. When there came before them a choice between stripes, persecution, and death, or compliance with the sense of duty, Peter said, in no vain boasting, knowing his own weakness, " Whether it be right to hearken unto you rather than to God, judge ye." He appealed to their consciences and to ours, that the voice of duty takes precedence of every other consideration; that we cannot escape from it; that it is the voice of God; that our duty and happiness are forever inseparable. It is the purpose of God and Christianity that we should always yield to duty. Let us, then, when we look into this religion of grace, remember that it is grace only that law may be fulfilled. And you will observe that this is provided for in the philosophy of the Christian religion. It is not a philosophy of forgiveness by fiat. It is not a religion which leads men to look up to heaven that forgiveness may come by words, but a religion that works according to unchanging and unalterable laws within us, — laws which tell us that the will of God cannot be escaped.

You take the Holy Sacrament upon your lips, and you make the most solemn oath that you will never flinch from duty or shrink from obligation; that you will never hesitate to do whatever God enjoins upon you. And this is a religion of freedom and gladness because it is a religion of law, — law which coincides with your own deepest desires and aspirations.

If such, then, be the right conception, duty is only another name for love. The sense of duty is only one side of a sense of love that springs up where there is a consciousness of forgiveness.

> "Stern Law-Giver, yet Thou dost wear
>   The Godhead's most benignant grace.
> Nor know we anything so fair
>   As is the smile upon Thy face.
> Flowers laugh before Thee on their beds,
> And fragrance in Thy footing treads.
> Thou dost preserve the stars from wrong,
> And the most ancient heavens through Thee are fresh and strong.
>
> "To humbler functions, awful Power,
>   Thee we call. We ourselves commend
> Unto Thy guidance from this hour.
>   O may our weakness have an end.

> Give unto us, made lowly wise,
> The spirit of self-sacrifice.
> The confidence of wisdom give,
> And through the light of truth Thy bondmen let us live."

Young Gentlemen of the Graduating Class: Your college life is now ending. Its opportunities, neglected or improved, are all gone to return no more forever. Its honors have all been won or lost. The record of your college life is written on your characters, intellectual and moral, in lines never to be effaced. There are epochs in the life of every individual as there are also in nations, — periods of transition; points from which there is an opportunity for retrospection and anticipation. You look back with something of gratification upon the four years that you have been associated together. They have been years of more than ordinary class prosperity. No root of bitterness has sprung up to disturb your fellowship. You have dwelt in harmony, and you have had more than the usual prosperity of college classes. Your honors have not been easily won. You have done well. You have profound reason for gratitude to God, — gratitude for the preservation of your numbers. One only has fallen by the way, — one the manliest among the manly. His aspirations were all high and pure. Uncorrupted in principle and animated by honest ambition to prepare himself for unusually responsible trusts that awaited him, your classmate, Sayles, finished his course in your second year. Disease smote him; Death claimed him for his own. Unrepiningly, patiently, trustingly he laid himself down to die, and God took him. May your careers be as noble and unspotted as his. There is a future before you. No one of you knows to what the paths on which you are about to enter will lead you. There is something mysterious, something grand, something inspiring, something almost awful, if I may so call it, in the career of a young man who bids adieu to college life and starts out into the great race of society. Hidden dangers, unexpected temptations, trials and burdens will come to you. You know not, any one of you, how high you may go, how great the trusts that will be committed to you. How many and anxious the hopes that will centre in you, God knows. Let me tell you, young gentlemen, there is but one Being that can know. To Him you can go with confidence. You cannot tell the secrets of your hearts even to your nearest fellow; even if you would he cannot know them. There is an eye that reads the subtilest thought, and knows it before it is your own; and He alone can keep you and strengthen you and nerve you to manliness, and make you quit yourselves like men.

Let me commend to you that upon which we have tried to dwell, — the sense of duty.

> "Its slightest touches, instant pause;
> Debar a' side pretences
> And resolutely keep its laws,
> Uncaring consequences."

There will be consequences. Men may sneer to hear you refuse to do evil. There are men that may laugh and deride when you dare to stand up in the face of society and say: " I dare not do evil; " when you say in the weakness of your own spirit, but in the strength of the divine Helper: "I dare to do right." There may be great consequences in this. The consequences are that the very men who scorned you will be the first to trust you. Never forget that any success in life, won by disloyalty to truth and disregard to duty, will be a fatal defeat; that any gain, wrought by a sacrifice of duty, will be a fatal loss. And, young gentlemen, looking upon you with something of a father's heart, may God keep you. Let me, above all things, remind you that our holy religion, at which so many venture in our day publicly to scoff, is the sole hope of man; and that He who taught men how to live and how to die, and how to triumph, will keep you if you trust Him, and help you to triumph as He did. May you know what it is to be humble, faithful servants of God and disciples of Jesus Christ. Amen.

SCIENCE AND THE CHRISTIAN RELIGION.

What is the Almighty that we should serve Him? and what profit should we have if we pray unto Him?

JOB xxi. 15.

THESE words sound as if they might have been written yesterday, rather than three thousand years ago. They embody questions with which our ears are every day becoming increasingly familiar. They are questions which are asked with an eagerness of tone that startles Christendom. The conception of a personal God is now openly assailed on the two grounds, — first, that if there be a God, it is impossible to assure ourselves that we know what kind of a being He is; and, secondly, assuming that He is what the Bible represents Him to be, the personal character which the popular Biblical religion is producing is in no way superior, but in fact is inferior to that which the Gospel of natural science is now giving to the world.

Whether we can know what God is, or not, it is plain enough that we may know what His worshippers are; and if we know what His worshippers are, it is not difficult to determine what their notions of Him must be, and we may safely leave it to the common sense of mankind to decide whether their notions be just and God in Himself really is what He is supposed to be.

The aim of all true religion manifestly must be to assist man in attaining to the highest end for which he exists; and one end for which he exists, it is equally manifest, must be the free, full, and harmonious development of every faculty of his being. No higher end is possible without this. So far, therefore, as we fall short of this end, and so far as we fail of any one of the successive steps by which this end is reached, life becomes a failure. And any form of religion which contents itself with mere abstinences, mortifications, and humiliations, or which prompts only to protestations of faith and love, without the fruits of righteous living, is not a religion which can either prove itself to be divine or can command the respect of honest and reflecting minds. True religion will not end in mere negations; it will not merely save a man from his fears and his penalties; it will not leave him alone till it has made the most and the best of him of which he is capable. The surest test, therefore, of the truth of a religion is the kind of character into which it moulds its adherents.

And it is equally clear that a man's conduct and character will be simply what his innermost convictions make them. Ascertain what his strongest convictions really are, and you may know for a certainty what his character must be. Determine what his character really is, and you may affirm with assurance what his hidden convictions are. A man's strongest convictions and deepest desires may antagonize at the first. The struggle between them may be protracted and deadly, but the convictions, if enlightened and established, will prevail. The two in the end will coalesce and be one. The man will become what his convictions make him. "As a man thinketh in his heart so is he." Trace his words and his deeds to their origin, and they will be found to spring from what, in his deepest heart, he believes to be truest and best. And his words and his deeds, as a whole, will be identical with what he in himself really is. His being and his doing will be but the two sides of one indivisible whole, and the informing principle of the whole will be the faith that rules him.

In the existing conflict between science and religion, which certain persons are greatly disposed to exaggerate, intimations have been broadly given that a comparison of the characters of the leading men of science in our time with the characters of the most typical representatives of the Christian religion, would be to the honor of science rather than of Christianity.

Let it be our present task to recognize briefly and fairly the good offices which science is capable of rendering in the great work of building up manhood and virtue in the earth, but also to point out, with equal fairness, its total incapacity to take the place and do the work of the religion of Jesus Christ.

Natural science is doubtless specially favorable to the cultivation of some of the primary elements of a noble character. And they are elements which are all the more necessary because, being primary, they are often overlooked. But as there can be no language without an alphabet, so there can be no just and symmetrical character without its elementary ingredients. Some of even the most needed of these, science can contribute.

Thus the very beginning of all true personal worth lies

in a supreme regard for truth as truth, — a willingness to sacrifice every thought and purpose of one's being at its shrine. This all-conquering love for truth as truth, science, it is claimed, imparts as one of its first gifts to its votaries. And undoubtedly the very soul of science is an insatiable inquisitiveness after fact and reality. Science never sits down with conjecture; it will not dwell content under the roof of hypothesis; it will not tarry in its course till it stands face to face with reality. Literature lets her votaries dally with fancy; lets them do the unworthy work of sophistry; lets them follow with equal complacency in the trains of truth or of error. But science inspires with scorn for whatever is unreal and for whatever would detain or divert us from the pursuit and ascertainment of reality and truth. No wonder, then, that the devotees of science should also be devotees, and martyrs even, to what they conceive to be truth; should prove themselves to be pre-eminently possessors of this first and most distinctive of all the elements of a high and praiseworthy character.

Akin to a love of truth as truth, is truthfulness toward one's self. A reverent love for truth exacts also a rigorous honesty in dealing with one's self. A thorough-going honesty of both purpose and act in the discipline of self is an ingredient without which no character can be either praiseworthy or complete. To the supply of this ingredient, true science is necessarily tributary. No man can habituate himself to the study of the invariable order of sequences in nature and not feel that, above all things else, he must not deceive himself nor allow himself to be deceived.

Again, natural science has it in its power to originate and nurture in the soul a third great element of all true nobility of character,— namely, an inflexibility of purpose which no bribe of gain nor blandishment of sense can seduce into disloyalty to the true and the right. To the eye of science, nature reveals herself as uniform in all her movements, as inexorable in all her laws, as holding together the universe in an unchanging order, as moving ever onward in her silent and resistless courses, before which the cry of the strongest is as unavailing as the wail of a new-born infant. Can any one spend his life in watching these forces, in studying the boundless and unchanging order which they produce and conserve, and himself not be schooled into habitudes of enduring purpose and character?

The pursuits of science, furthermore, are captivating, and leave no taste for objects that degrade and demoralize. They are engrossing, and leave no time for pursuits that distract the thoughts and waste the energies. The love of science leaves no room in the soul for the play of the baser passions; it deafens the ear to the clamor of the appetites; it lifts a man up to a plane of life whither the vices of the vulgar herd cannot climb. To plant in the heart, therefore, a true love for science, is to impart a power which almost insures to its possessor some of the manliest of the human virtues.

The virtues which the lessons of science inculcate, it must be admitted, are only virtues of the homelier and the sturdier classes. But they are virtues which the popular philosophy and the popular religion of our time have not been notably successful in cultivating. They are virtues to which sentimentalists in philosophy and religion do not attach the highest importance, which emotional religion is always disposed to neglect or to depreciate. And for these very reasons they are virtues which this generation all the more needs to have thrust on its attention. We need to be taught that there are sterner and more manly virtues than sentimentalism and emotional religion is disposed in our time to cultivate.

But who shall tell us to what extent there is indebtedness, for even these few homely virtues, to the indirect and incidental influence of the very religion which it is proposed to supplant? What nation is there, within which science now exists and flourishes, whose intellectual firmament is not so studded with the great moral truths which Christianity alone has placed there, that no man can, if he would, escape their light? When once the atmosphere of the Christian moralities has fallen on a people, there is no walk in life to which it does not penetrate; no class or rank who do not breathe it, and none of its educated men, who, dealing honestly with themselves, and striving manfully after the truth, do not inhale it and are not strengthened by it.

And supposing a belief in the divine authority of Christianity could be overthrown? What then? Would science become independent of the Gospel of Christ?

The influence of a religion remains long after a regard for it as divine has ceased. The odor of the vase survives in its fragments and lingers long in its powdered dust. Were the Bible to be thrown aside to-day as a book of fables; were Christianity to be henceforth treated as a religion of human device; were pulpits to be dumb, churches to be closed, and the hope of immortality to perish, — centuries would not suffice for the influence of the religion of the Bible to die out. The golden threads of its thoughts are so wrought into the whole web of our modern civilization that demons could not pick them all out though they tore that web into shreds, though they accomplished the disintegration and downfall of society itself.

In short, a test of what physical science alone can accomplish morally for man is, in this generation, and in any Christian land, a simple impossibility. Indeed, it is more than probable that the test never can be made. Thus far it has been in Christian lands alone that physical science has existed, not to say flourished; and there are the best of reasons for believing that the ethical truths of Christianity — truths which Christianity alone gave to the race — shall yet be recognized by all science and religion alike as the first truths and the first principles of all true morality, truths which underlie this universe, truths which will not be dependent on Christianity even for their support, but which, once given to the race, are to be so universally proclaimed and so inwrought into all human thinking that science itself can never escape them.

But not alone to its influence on the personal character of individuals have the good offices of natural science been restricted. Its services to ethics and theology, those great systems of thought which in centuries past have shaped the character and determined the destiny of nations, are still more conspicuous. Natural science has brought us to look for and to find the eternal truths imbedded in those great metaphors by which alone the most fundamental truths of religion and morals could be announced to men, but to which popular thinking has been perpetually disposed to give literal interpretations. It was a most ungracious but most needful service which Titus wrought in destroying the Temple at Jerusalem, and in taking away forever its golden candlesticks. Not less useful and not less ungracious is the service which physical science is now rendering in pulling down some venerable structure, built of metaphors and figures of speech, under which good men, it may be, like pious Jews in their loved Temple, have long worshipped sincerely, but which, having served its purpose, we need not now lament to see removed. Physical science is teaching us that moral laws are not mere decretive precepts, the sanctions of which can be enforced or remitted at will, but that they are eternal principles of being which are as immutable as the nature of God; that if moral law be broken, its penalty cannot be remitted by fiat; that God will not violate His moral law to save any one; that He will Himself be just or He will not justify the sinner. It has taught men that personal character can no more be a matter of literal imputation than personal identity can be changed, than wrong can be made right by a change of words, or than error can be made truth by calling it so. Science is teaching this generation that a religion which is true, and which is to command the homage of men, must deal with realities and not with fictions; must show its power in the construction of enduring character, and not expend itself in mere words and obtrusive professions of belief.

And all these are offices which science is capable of performing, which it has performed and is now performing for men; and for men some of whom assure us with a melancholy pride that they can find no trace of a Creator, or of a Supreme Being, in any part of the universe to which they have yet been able to gain access. They tell us that to them the heavens are empty; that the only voices which salute their ears amid the solitudes of nature are the inarticulate sounds of colliding and mechanical forces; that the only thought which nature's ten thousand adaptations of means to ends suggest to them is that of the uniformity of law, according to which blind and inscrutable force works ever onward and onward, aimless and undirected, and yet producing a universe of intelligible and perfect order.

But granting now, as we may, all that can be claimed for natural science in its clarification of our moral and religious ideas, and especially in its cultivation of the virtues, civic, social, or personal — and Heaven forbid that a syllable escape us in disparagement of aught it can accomplish, or that we should join in an insane clamor against all morality and virtue which are not the growth of our special teachings — the question still remains whether there be a single one of all human virtues which the Christian religion does not more effectually cultivate; whether, after all that science can accomplish for man, he is not, without Christianity and the personal Christ, so radically deficient as to be helpless and hopeless when tried in the balances in which science itself would weigh him? Let us look at particulars.

Natural science instils into the heart of its students

a reverent love for truth as truth. And does not the first lesson of Christianity teach man to look through illusions to realities? Does it not insist that if a man be not willing to sacrifice himself even, if need be, for the truth's sake, it is because the love of truth is not in him. And more than all, it is not alone the truths of things, or of any narrow range of knowledge, but all truth in the universe of beings as well as of things, which Christianity bids us seek, and bids us love, and bids us make ourselves possessors of at any hazard and at any sacrifice. Science contents itself with phenomena and their laws; the Christian religion pierces all phenomena to ascertain the truths that lie within them. Both glory in truth; but the one rests in the truth of inanimate matter; the other deals with the truths of both matter and spirit.

But here we shall be told that science accepts nothing as truth which has not the test of experience, while religion accepts on authority and tradition. The one, it is said, talks only of what it knows; the other, of what it believes. The one deals with laws; the other with dogmas; and ecclesiastical dogmas, we are told by a living historian and critic, are destructive to morality. But dogmas are the work of men and not of Christianity proper, the decrees of councils and not of God. Galileo was compelled to deny what he knew to be true, not by the Gospel of Christ, but by ignorant and impertinent ecclesiastics. The divine command is, "Prove all things and hold fast that which is good." A professed belief in what has not been intelligently accepted is a mockery, a delusion, and a snare. A pretended belief in a dogma which does not command the assent of both the understanding and the heart, is fatal alike to all true morality and all true virtue. But Christianity demands our assent, not to dogmas, but to truth, and leaves no soul at rest till assured that truth has been found.

Again, honesty with one's self, that corner-stone of all worthy character, is also specially claimed as one of the gifts of science to man. And who shall be faithful to himself, and honest in the innermost secrets of his heart, if not he who consciously walks under the gaze of an omniscient eye and hourly speaks to Him from whom no shadow of a thought can be hidden. Under Christian tuition it is not law which makes a man honest and reverent towards himself, but the Lawgiver, in whose image himself was made. It is not the fear of penalty which makes him severely just in his treatment of himself, but an abiding sense of that eternal Presence before which insincerity flees as darkness before the light.

And yet again, if natural science ministers to inflexibility of purpose and to a wholesome hardihood of character, it is because these are the hourly lessons taught by the inexorability of natural law. But if mere law can teach this effectually, how much more shall the eternal mind, that through the law proclaims its unchanging purpose? If blind mechanical force, working unalterably in its courses, can persuade the human intelligence to steadiness of purpose and to persistency of action, how much more if that force proclaims an intelligent and unchanging will? And if physical law can do all this, how much more can the moral? The Founder of our holy religion taught both by words and in His own person the inexorability of moral law. The heavens and the earth, said He, may pass away, but one jot or tittle of the law can in no wise fail. The very spirit of His religion is the spirit of patient endurance, of a courage that never falters, of a stability of hope and heart and character which cannot be moved. Where will you look for fixedness of purpose, for stability of character, for the highest of human virtues that this world knows, if not in him whose hopes are built on the immutable promises of an immutable God?

But enough of all this. It seems like an offence against the intelligence of a Christian audience to be defending the influence on the character of a belief in the existence of a personal God, as against belief in a merely impersonal force of nature; like solemn trifling to attempt vindication of the superiority of Christian morality and virtue as compared with the virtue and morality which the mere laws of matter would inculcate. That such vindication and defence have become possible, not to say necessary, before a Christian audience, is proof enough, not only of the presumption of science, but of the sad deficiencies in the style of character too often produced by the popular religion of our day.

But turn us for a moment to a closer inspection of the moral handiwork of science. Let us look at the boasted excellence of character which it is capable of producing. Select an ideally perfect specimen. And what have we? The absence of all vices; a loving loyalty to truth; an honesty as transparent as light; a devotion to science that borders on the spirit of martyrdom. These are great and praiseworthy virtues. And could science alone produce them, then were they jewels in her crown. But Christianity produces them, produces them of the highest type, and, in fact, first taught the world to appreciate them at their true value. But they do not constitute the whole of human virtue; nor are they the most difficult of acquisition. There are the finer virtues, which mark the gentleman, which adorn the citizen, which grace the husband and father, which make the humble, self-distrustful, self-denying servant of God, disciple of Christ, and "lover of all good men;" these are virtues which require another light and atmosphere to grow in than physical science can furnish. And more than all are those subtile and still finer virtues of the heart, the gentleness, meekness, sweetness, purity, and peace which only the practised eye discerns, which reveal themselves only in the closest intimacies of life, and which only the supreme worship and love of Him in whom all attributes unite and are perfected, can produce in the soul. These are virtues of which science knows nothing, and which, untutored by an intelligence higher than itself, it would trample underfoot. These virtues, too refined for its rude test of utility, it relegates to sentiment, and to sentiment which itself is totally incompetent to create. But all these are virtues which are distilled, like the dew on the flowers, by the very atmosphere of the religion of Christ.

It may be that the Stoicism of ancient heathenism, revived by modern science, may have a temporary resurrection, but it can never permanently take the place of the religion of Jesus Christ. Nothing which fails to satisfy every yearning of the human heart can command the abiding homage of the human soul. But the song of the Christian is, —

> "Thou, O Christ, art all I want;
> More than all in Thee I find."

And every new believer takes up the song with as much freshness of feeling as if he had been the first to discover its truth.

But even supposing that the elect few who are admitted to the mysteries of science, can find in its teachings, as they claim, all that the human soul needs, how about the great multitudes of men on whom the light of science falls only by a faint and reflected radiance? The few high priests of nature whose pursuits withdraw them from the haunts of men, who dwell upon the high table-lands of thought apart from the turmoils of society, may be seen from afar, conspicuous examples of the manly virtues. They may proclaim abroad that they have diligently sought for the Christian's God, but cannot find Him; that Jesus Christ is not their Saviour; that they have saved themselves. The vast crowds of men who people the lower plains of common life hear the proclamation: "The Christian's God has vanished; the Christian religion is a fiction; death is an eternal sleep; the resurrection a cheat, and immortality a lie." "Filthy dreamers," self-styled scientists, catch up the sounding words, spring to the street corners and shout to the passers-by that the institutions of religion are an incubus to society; that marriage is a cruel yoke; that the existing laws of morality are not the laws of nature but of priestcraft; that men are not free, but the victims of superstition.

Communists hear the cry, and with louder shouts denounce wealth as robbery, capitalists as pirates, religion as a fraud, the churches as in league with tyranny, and all modern society as so corrupt that nothing but a universal baptism of blood can cleanse it. Have the heralds of the new Evangel counted on those followers that will flock to their standards? — can they fail to foresee the results of their teachings? Can that be truth which leads to such issues? Is it to such issues that we in these last days are coming?

No! it is not moral chaos and blank despair to which we are hastening. Nature herself will repudiate the priests that belie her. The eternal and invisible God whom nature conceals while it reveals Him, and who has never " left Himself without witness" on the earth, will bring to confusion the false prophets, and in His own time and way will make Himself to be heard and to be revered. It is not science, but ignorance that asks " what is the Almighty that we should serve Him, and what profit should we have if we pray unto Him?" Even now " Wisdom crieth without; she uttereth her voice in the streets; she crieth in the chief places of concourse, in the openings of the gates; in the city she uttereth her words, saying, How long, ye simple ones, will ye love simplicity, and the scorners delight in their scorning, and fools hate knowledge?" And more than all, there is a voice in the depths of every human soul, which the din of life may drown for awhile, but which, sooner or later, will make itself heard, — a voice that " crieth out for the living God." There is in every human heart a yearning which passion, or the pride of opinion, may long suppress, but which, when the light of life begins to grow dim, and the deepening shadows to fall thick and fast, will break out in the articulate cry, —

> "O, somewhere, somewhere, God unknown,
> Exist and be!
> I am dying; I am all alone;
> I must have Thee."

And that which gives to this cry its great bitterness is the conscious presence in the soul of a power which hides the very Being who is called upon. It is a power which corrupts the affections, which enfeebles the will, and which binds in fetters that the soul of itself can never break. It is a power to which every human being has yielded obedience, and yet a power for obedience to which every human being arraigns himself at a tribunal from which there can be no appeal. Betrayed, enslaved, and self-condemned, it is in vain that the soul appeals to natural science for relief. Science mocks the soul in its agony by telling it to be patient and strong. To every cry for help and remedy, science scornfully replies, "There is no help nor remedy which the soul does not itself possess; man must save himself or perish." Wounded and bleeding, the soul is flung back to its anguish and death. But till the power of moral evil in the soul be broken, till the heart be cleansed, till the sense of sin be washed out by the blood of Christ, till the wounds of the spirit be bound up and healed, till man be renewed in the spirit and temper of his mind, no peace, no symmetry nor rounded beauty of character for him are possible. Surely that is a "saying worthy of all acceptation, that Jesus Christ came into the world to save sinners."

Nothing in human history is more distinctive or conspicuous than the evidence of the universal sense of guilt. The earth has groaned with altars and temples erected for its appeasement. Human blood has been freely poured out to wash it away. Schemes of philosophy and religion have been devised for its removal. The heavens have re-echoed with piercing cries for release from it. But all in vain, except as men have listened to the words from heaven: "He that calleth on the name of the Lord shall be saved." The only science or philosophy that has ever built men up in righteousness and true holiness is the science and philosophy of redemption through a crucified Saviour. "This is eternal life, to know Thee the only true God and Jesus Christ whom Thou hast sent."

Gentlemen of the Graduating Class: The characters you have been forming, both mental and moral, are now to pass under the review of other eyes than those which have been carefully watching them for the four years past. You will be scrutinized, and it will soon be discovered what manner of persons you are.

On the characters you have been acquiring will depend, more than you can now understand, your future careers. Foundations have been laid; on these you must build. No man can build for you; the structures must be your own. And what shall the structures be? The question is pertinent to the place and the hour.

Mistakes have doubtless been committed in your

college life; days have been lost which can never be recalled; opportunities neglected which can never be repeated. In all this you have but shared the common lot of youthful humanity. Some good habits of both mind and heart have also undoubtedly been formed. You will be wise men if you let the past teach you a right use of the future. Towards that use, listen for a moment to a parting word of counsel.

Remember, first of all, that the one aim of life, to which all others should be subordinated, is the acquisition of such character, mental, moral, and religious, as shall stand approved of God and not condemned of yourselves. Without this, the greater your other successes in life, the swifter, surer, and deeper will be your doom. With this, the freedom of the universe will be yours; the presence of God will be your final home, and the resources of infinite love will be at your service.

But neither God nor yourself can approve any character which is not founded on eternal truth and on immutable right, which is only another name for truth in its relation to life. Cherish, therefore, as you will your own lives, a love for truth simply as truth. This love, feeble at first, will strengthen with your strength, will arm you with its might, will keep you erect and faithful, while others, faithless, will falter and fall. And in your search for truth, remember that not all is true which is new, and not all is antiquated which is ancient. What good men, wise and faithful, have through the changing centuries found by experience to be unchanging truth to them, you may safely assume will, if intelligently tested, prove to be truth to you.

Next to the love of truth, cherish the habit of scrupulous honesty in judging yourselves. Self-conceit is a sign of despicable weakness; pride and self-complacency are signs of still more despicable vanity and self-flattery, and so of dishonesty. He who knows himself thoroughly and judges himself justly, will be likely to hold himself at a lower estimate than others can. At any rate, when the final rewards of life shall be distributed, he will have the pleasure of being bidden to a higher, rather than the mortification of being thrust down to a lower, seat than he had judged to be his due.

So, also, finally, settle it now, once for all and forever, that, come what may, you will always dare to do right. Remember that a success obtained by any species of deception is a failure, and a failure which eternity cannot repair; that a refusal to do wrong is a triumph, and a triumph the results of which eternity cannot exhaust.

You enter active life at a time when truth and error, right and wrong, righteousness and iniquity are in the closest and deadliest conflict. Leave no one in doubt on which side you enlist. Rest assured in yourselves that truth and right and righteousness will prevail. Clouds and darkness may sweep over the face of society for a day, but justice and judgment are on the throne above the clouds, and in due time will be established in the habitations of men. Let no man nor devil, therefore, beguile you for an instant from your loyalty to truth, to righteousness, and to God.

You will be tried; temptations will assail you; no mortal escapes them. The question is, Will you resist them and be victors, or succumb to them and be slaves? Trusting in your own strength, you will yield, and yielding, you will despise yourselves and be despised by others. Trusting in Him who, alone of all that have walked this earth, was tempted without sin, you will be victors in this world, and receive a crown of life in the world to come.

THE RIGHT AIM IN LIFE.

It is written, man shall not live by bread alone, but by every word that proceedeth out of the mouth of God.

MATTHEW iv. 4.

EVERY man in this world comes, sooner or later, to a point where his way divides itself into an indefinite number of paths, some one of which he must select for the remainder of his journey. This point, however, is not reached by all men at the same period of life. Sometimes a kindly Providence apparently shapes everything for a man at the moment of his birth. Not till some sudden calamity overwhelms him is he roused into a conscious necessity of deciding for himself what he will do and become. He was dropped into a niche where he reposed long years without thought or care, till some rude shock threw him into the dusty arena of life, when, compelled to do or die, he first decided upon the principles which made his conduct and his character his own. But to most men there comes early in life the occasion and the necessity for deliberation and decision. An educated man is ordinarily brought to his day of deliberation and choice at his graduation from college. A goal is then reached from which a new start is to be taken in life. Towards what goal in the future, he then asks, shall I now direct my steps, and by what route and methods shall it be reached? To each of these questions he is forced to give himself some kind of answer. To assist those who here to-day have these questions before them, to give answers which they may never regret, is the object of this discourse.

What, then, is the worthiest aim in life? What purpose is that which, towering above all others, should subject every other to itself? To what final summing up of life ought a rational being to look calmly and steadily forward? What end ought a mind, supposed to have been enlightened and refined by a liberal education, to set before itself as the one comprehensive object of its unfaltering pursuit?

To earn an honest livelihood is certainly one end in life, and not an unworthy one. To idle away one's days is to wrong one's self, and to sin against God and mankind. But man cannot live by bread alone. Mere livelihood is but a foundation without a structure. One must subsist to accomplish any end; but to be content with subsisting without aiming at many and harmonious ends which can be rounded into a completed whole, is to subsist unworthily and to make life a comparative failure.

Man stands connected with this world by innumerable ties, and every tie is an obligation which cannot be severed, however much it may be neglected. Every obligation understood is a word of God to man, and every obligation fulfilled ministers vigor to the soul. Honest and persistent endeavors to fulfil all the obligations of life bring the serenest joy and the completest life that man can know. The highest, purest, and worthiest life for man is not to attempt to live by bread alone, but by every word that proceedeth out of the mouth of God; and thus, in fact, to make the utmost possible of himself of which he is capable.

Nor is this a selfish aim. To make the utmost possible of one's self is to do the utmost possible in the service of both God and man. To rise towards one's ideal is to do one's daily duties. The ideal man is the man in whom no virtue is wanting, because no duty has been neglected.

The connection of man's duties with his character is an inseparable one, and never to be lost sight of. Too often they are conceived as divisible, and sometimes even as opposites. As if any man could ever really be otherwise than what he actually does; as if being and doing were anything else than two stages of one and the same thing. The truth is, duties exist for man and not man for his duties. All ordinances of God, all just laws of men, are for the improvement of man. Jesus Christ Himself came down from heaven to earth for the sole purpose of making men godlike. The supreme purpose of our holy religion is to enable man, under the two-fold discipline of law and grace, of duty and love, to make the utmost possible of himself as a rational and a religious being. No worthier purpose can any man set before himself in this world or any other, than to lift himself up by the grace of God, just as fast and just as high as he can towards a realization of the highest type of his race; not to lift himself into places of power, of emolument, and of self-glorification, but into the possession of real and imperishable worth. The best of men

"Are those of whom the noisy world hears least,"

and who, it may be added, care least for the noisy world's applause.

Let us look, now, for a moment, at the reasons which may be adduced for the aim in life which we have proposed. To aim at this is to aim at the fulfilment of every obligation in life. To succeed in it, will be to fill the whole sphere of human duty.

According to the best of catechisms, the soundest of philosophies and theologies, and the plain teachings of Scripture, the foremost duty of man is to glorify his Maker. Nor can science prove the contrary. What see we in the flowers beneath our feet and in the heavens above our heads? The glory of the laws of mechanics and of chemistry, or the glory of the wisdom and goodness, of the order and beauty, of the Eternal Mind that works by law? But what the heavens and the earth do as the handiwork of God, man is to do as the image of God. The more exact the image, the more complete the glorification of the original. "Herein is My Father glorified, that ye bear much fruit." The higher one rises towards the Christian ideal of manhood, the more effectually does he proclaim the glory of the Creator of man. A nation of high-souled men, with characters pure, stable, and symmetrical, would be an epistle from God for the eyes of the universe.

Indeed, any attempt, intelligently made, to fill out a Christian ideal of life will prompt to the glory of God. Summon the forces of your being and attempt to subject them to your purpose; step forth into the world resolved to beat down temptation and to overcome evil, and you will speedily find that a godless spirit in a godless world can accomplish any end rather than that of the ideal life of a Christian. If honest in your attempt, you will find yourself forced into the petitions, " Give us this day our daily bread. And forgive us our trespasses as we forgive those who trespass against us. And lead us not into temptation, but deliver us from evil, for Thine is the kingdom, the power, and the glory, for ever and ever."

A second duty of man is self-control and a willing humiliation of self to the Will that rules the universe. This is man's hardest lesson; and this is the lesson which the aim in life now urged, honestly cherished, forces him first of all to learn. This teaches him, at the outset, how helpless and hopeless he is in himself. No knowledge humbles a man in his own sight like this; and none, rightly used, leads so directly to his exaltation. Such knowledge drives a man out of himself hungry and thirsty for every word that proceedeth out of the mouth of God, and especially for the word that shall enable him to " keep his own heart," out of which are the issues of life. When once he has learned to lay hold of the Power which alone can help him, then begins the process which ends in the mastery of self and in the consummation of a life which alone is worth living. " Greater is he that ruleth his own spirit than he that taketh a city."

Again, every man should be helpful to his fellowman, — should regard mankind as a universal brotherhood, whose welfare is to him a never-failing incentive to action. Nor will the aim to raise himself to the highest manhood make any one otherwise than mindful of the welfare of his race. Every healthy soul yearns for society as the river seeks the ocean. Between the individual and society the inlets and outlets of health or disease are as numerous and vital as are the powers and capacities of the soul. Like the tree of the forest, the roots of one's being are interlaced with the roots of every other being with whom he stands associated. No man, therefore, can discipline himself into nobleness of nature, into strength, largeness, and beauty of character, without taking into account what he owes to his fellowmen, as well as what he is ever receiving from them. He who absorbs and never imparts, delude himself as he may into the belief that his nature is expanding, is hourly dwarfing himself into a littleness which himself in due time will not fail to despise. But he who remembers men, and toils for them as well as for himself, never fails to find that to give is better than to receive, and that the surest method of lifting one's self upward is in lowly, self-forgetful helpfulness to others.

That no worthier object in life is possible for man than the perfectibility of his own character is evident from the capacities and laws of his being. Here both nature and revelation may teach us. Nature teaches that everything animate in this world is constituted after a plan, and everything, when the conditions of its life are duly supplied, strives ever upward toward the perfectibility of its type. Stingy as may be the soil from which the violet springs, harsh and cruel as may be the skies under which it opens its petals, it nevertheless strives ever towards perfection in its coloring, its fragrance, and its fruitage. Tear the mocking-bird from his native forest, cage him, shut him in your house, and saddening as his life is, he always does his utmost to sing his best. Nature everywhere struggles upward towards her perfect type. So also man, adverse as may be the circumstances of his birth, education, and associations, perverse as may be his hereditary impulses, depraved as he may be both by birth and by habit, finds himself ever reminded by the unchanging laws of his being of something nobler and worthier than his earth-born tastes are ever prompting him to seek. From these original laws of his being no amount of depravity can tear him away, and no amount of piety or of grace can ever absolve him. The demand of these laws is, that he shall never tarry in his course, or rest content with what he is. The something better than he has attained ever hovers above him, and every principle of his being prompts him to efforts to reach it.

To what nature, blind though it be, thus impels man, revelation clearly and emphatically invites him. The author of Christianity was Himself the type and pattern of perfect humanity. What Christ was as man, he taught that men could and ought to become. "I am come," said He, "that ye might have life, and that ye might have it more abundantly;" that ye might not only have life, but might know the secret of extracting the largest possible measure of life from every earthly duty and relation. Thus the first step of His holy religion to those who receive it, is to re-organize the forces of the soul, restoring every faculty to its legitimate office, and putting the whole personality upon a new career. Ideal humanity made real in the person of Christ is thus, in a degree, made possible for those who will receive from

Christ the power to attain to it. Nor is this all. "Now are we the sons of God, and it doth not yet appear what we shall be." A career of inconceivable dignity and compass is opened before us, and every one is invited to strive to his utmost to fit himself to enter upon it; and to quicken us in the strife there stands the assurance that the infinite resources of Godhead are pledged to our support. How low and vulgar and despicable seem the paltry baubles which men pursue, for which they sacrifice ease, honor, and conscience even, forgetful of what they are capable of becoming, and of what an infinitely gracious Creator destined and invites them to be.

Again, some kind of regard for one's own happiness must be taken into account in any comprehensive conception of the worthiest aim in life. God, history, and reason, alike, teach us to bethink ourselves and provide for this demand of our souls. The command of God is, "Thou shalt love thy neighbor as thyself," thus making a proper self-love to be at once the basis and the measure of the love due to others. And reason teaches us that to be and to delight in being, naturally co-exist, — that a healthy soul craves the blessedness of existence as naturally as the lungs crave the atmosphere; that we might as well attempt to think of a watch without a mainspring, of a plant without life, or of an animal without instincts, as of a human being without the desire of happiness. And history teaches us that any attempt, under whatever guise of piety and religion, to extinguish or to ignore the soul's instinctive desire for its own happiness, is sure to be avenged sooner or later by an outbreak of that desire in forms that mar and make hideous what God designed to be beautiful and lovely.

But of all the happiness which man can know, none is more refining or more inspiring than that which springs from the consciousness of personal improvement. As when one climbs a height, the higher he ascends, the purer the air he breathes and the wider and more inspiriting the scene that opens around him. Each new stage reached renews his energy for another and a higher.

The influence of such a life as we are pleading for is plainly seen in any community where it may be lived. One such life is a healthful power over a wide circle. Like some lofty mountain with its unfailing mantle of snow, it is an inspiring object to distant beholders, and sends down its cooling currents to refresh and invigorate the dwellers on the dusty plains below. Ten men living such lives would have saved even Sodom from its overthrow. A nation of such in our day would soon put new life-blood into the veins of the race.

Of such men every age and nation has had its need; but in no nation and in no generation was that need ever greater than it now is in our own, and on no class of men was the duty of living such lives ever more imperative than it is on the educated men of these United States. In solving the great problem of self-government, at which as a people we now are so anxiously laboring, who, pray, shall be leaders, if not the educated men of the country? Who, pray, ought to be fitted to be leaders, if not the men whose minds have been enlarged by knowledge, whose faculties have been sharpened by discipline and criticism, who have traced the fall of nations that vices and crimes have exterminated, who have read the unchangeable laws of God as written on the scroll of history in letters of blood, and on the heart of man in letters of light?

But alas! alas! it is not knowledge, it is not disciplined intellect, it is not familiarity with the fall of nations, or with the laws of God, that can save us, or that we so much need, as it is high character, an integrity which no self-interest can bribe, a sense of honor and a love of truth and justice which no seduction can betray. The land already groans under the burden of educated perversity, of strong and disciplined intellects absorbed in money-getting, of great knowledge prostituted to unworthy ends, of great endowments and splendid acquisitions sold to uses that are plainly corrupting the heart of the nation. In no way can an American citizen more directly honor God or serve his country than by resolving to stand

> "Among innumerable false, unmoved,
> Unshaken, unseduced, unterrified."

And to permit

> "Nor number, nor example with him work
> To swerve from truth, or change his constant mind
> Though single."

Let the action of a great convention of American citizens instruct us. Scheming politicians had long and warily laid their plans; partisanship had exhausted itself of its devices; the cunning and craft of politicians seemed on the eve of triumph. But to the honor of our common country be it said, that once and again have machine politics been wrecked, and wily demagogues been mutually outwitted. And more than all, the worth of an unimpeached and an unimpeachable character, the priceless value of untarnished honor and of unswerving fidelity to principle and duty, have been recognized in the selection of a candidate for the highest honor in the gift of fifty millions of people. There is yet hope for the republic.

Another result from a more general aspiration after high character would be a lifting up of the so-called learned professions from the low level to which they are constantly in danger of sinking. The taunt already is that the learned professions are degraded into trades; that the lawyer sells his briefs and his legal instruments as the marketman sells his steaks and the tailor his coats; that the doctor is more intent on the state of his ledger than on establishing his right to be called, in any sense, a good physician; that even the minister of the Gospel is more disposed to be content with his perfunctory sermons, baptisms, marriages, and funerals, than eager to prove himself a fitting ambassador from God to man; and they might add that the teacher, the professor in the higher institution of learning, is in danger of droning through his dreary lessons, forgetting that the best work can be done only by himself becoming an example and an inspiration to his pupils.

Nor is the motive which we thus urge for high endeavors in life, unworthy either the day, the place, or the occasion. Our callings in life, whether we will receive it or not, are by the vocation of God. Indivisible from one another are our callings and our characters. Thorough work in one will insure faithful work in the other. Thorough-going honesty in our callings is sure to react to the integrity and solidity and symmetry of our characters; and for our callings and our characters alike we shall find ourselves compelled at the last to give account both to ourselves and to God.

Again, were the acquisition of high personal virtue made the supreme aim in life, more commonly than it now is, it would do something towards relieving the prevailing religion of our day from one grave indictment brought against it. The doctrine of salvation by faith and grace, it is claimed, fails to produce the highest type of manhood; that, as commonly taught, it makes men more intent on escaping the consequences of sin than it does on aspiring to the eternal awards of virtue; that to be a Christian in our day is no guaranty of an integrity above that of the rest of mankind. The reproach lies in the apparent truth of the charges. But the fault is not in the doctrine, but in the one-sided statement of it. Here, as always, a half-truth is a whole error. In whom do we believe if not in Him who alone of all the beings who ever trod this earth was the perfect man? And what is faith, if not a power that tranforms into a likeness to the object of our trust? And what does Christianity more need to-day, in the pulpit, on the street, in the counting-room, at the bar, at the fireside, than truer illustrations of what Christianity is designed to accomplish for man as a denizen of this world, as well as a candidate for glory in another? In no way is Christianity more misrepresented than by the pinched and shrivelled type of piety presented by many who claim to be its only just expounders. And in no way can Christianity be so effectually commended to the intelligent minds of this observing and thinking age, as by putting before it, in living example, the best that Christianity can accomplish.

Again, to aim at making the utmost possible of one's self in life, is to be forearmed against a fatal despair. One of the startling things of this day of Christian enlightenment is the rapidly growing number of suicides. Not alone the infidel and the atheist, but the avowed believer in God and His Christ, is among them. In vain do you denounce them as craven-hearted cowards, as criminals in the sight of God and man. They would tell you, could they be summoned to testify, that they found life insupportable. And why? Simply because the little springs at which they sat down to drink had dried up. They had attempted to live by bread alone; and when it failed, despair seized them, and they rushed out of the world;

"hope died
And fear was lost in agony."

What now against this disease of despair can be made a sufficient and available safeguard? One answer is plain. Tie the man down, as you do the tent that is threatened by a storm, by guys that shall hold him firmly to the earth. Tell him that he must not live by bread alone, but by every word that proceedeth out of the mouth of God. Help him to see that every tie to earth is a duty enjoined of God; that the doing of every duty will be meat and drink to his soul; that the doing of all the duties of life, in the spirit and grace of Christ, will round him out into a contented and happy man. If you can help him to see and understand this, he is safe.

The question now arises, How can this great aim in life be made a real and effective purpose? Manifestly, first of all, there must be reflection. Ignorance is doubtless the fruitful mother of vices, but not of all.

> "Evil is wrought by want of thought
> As well as want of heart."

Knowledge is worthless in the guidance of life, without a just application of it; and a due application of it is impossible without thoughtfulness. And reflection should be at the beginning of life, or it may come too late.

A second requisite is, the remembrance that the laws of God and of our personal being are as unchangeable as God Himself, and that man can no more escape from them, or evade them, than he can escape from, or evade himself. Every part of the compound nature of man is bound to every other part by laws as unyielding as fate. Co-equal with the need of reflection, is the need of unshrinking submission to these laws. The body has its demands, and will not fail to avenge both neglect and abuse of itself. The mind, maltreated, curses and blights its possessor. And the fearful forces of that obscure realm of the emotions, the affections, the desires, and the volitions unrestrained by the rigid enforcement of law, rising in rebellion, overwhelm in hopeless ruin what was intended to be a temple of God. Without an eager desire, therefore, to know, and an unyielding purpose to comply with these laws of our three-fold nature,— laws so interlaced and inseparable in their action, and so inexorable in their several domains as to make man the most fearfully and wonderfully made of all the works of God,— there can be no approximation in any degree to the type of true manhood.

Another indispensable requisite unquestionably is, clear and settled convictions in respect to truth and duty. There is no disguising the fact that conflicting theories and systems of thought have shaken the confidence of many educated men in sundry traditional beliefs. It is evident enough, also, that a loss of confidence in some beliefs is fast generating a general spirit of indifference towards all positive religious truth. Doubt, distrust, and disbelief are becoming the distinguishing characteristics of our time. To cherish convictions which cost self-denial and bring one into collision with indifference and untruth is to expose one's self to the charge of narrow-mindedness, if not of bigotry. In the moral history of the race, we are threatened with a reversal of the historical order of the physical world, with a supplanting of moral vertebrates with moral mollusks. But without clear conceptions of the eternal verities of our being, without a conviction of their authority which no flattery nor blandishment can beguile, no character can be formed which will be worth the possessing. A character without a foundation of solid and settled convictions is a structure upon the sand. Living convictions, born of truths that set the souls of men aglow and astir, are the only forces that can lift up and carry forward this race of ours. I believe, said the Psalmist, and therefore speak. We believe and therefore speak, said the apostles of Jesus; and because the Psalmist believed and sang, and apostles believed, and spake, and acted, the starless and worn-out heavens of heathenism vanished, and the new heavens and the new earth of Christianity came to gladden the hearts of men.

One other requisite remains, without which all others are in vain. In every age men have tried the light of their own understandings, and it has misled them; they have relied on the strength of their own wills, and it has failed them. But who ever asked in sincerity the help of God, and his petition was denied to him? Who ever really trusted in Christ, and found that his faith had wrecked him on the shoals of error or on the rocks of vice? The words of Jesus are as true to-day as when He uttered them: "Without me ye can do nothing;" and the words of the apostle Paul are as true for us as they were for him: "I can do all things through Christ, who strengthens me." The root of all that is best and grandest in the achievement of the human soul is in its faith, and in strictest accordance with the object of its trust will always be the measure and the kind of what the soul achieves. Believing on the Son of God, man is not only saved from his sins and fears, from all that dwarfs and mars, but, renewed in the spirit and temper of his mind, he is put upon a career in which he need not stop till all shall be accomplished of which he is capable here, or which the Eternal Mind has prepared for him hereafter.

Gentlemen of the Graduating Class: The record of your college life has now been sealed up, and has gone forward to the great day of accounts. What your individual record has been, each of you knows for himself, and knows that it cannot now be altered. But what shall the record of your future be? What kind of aims do you propose to yourselves for the remainder of your lives? To these questions, consciously or unconsciously, you are here and now, under an omniscient eye, giving answer. Let the answers be such as you shall never desire to recall. That they may be wisely made, acquaint yourselves with God, and so be at peace with Him and at rest in yourselves. Then will you be able to see clearly, and to decide wisely; and having decided, to work with a spirit and a steadiness of purpose, without which nothing great or good can ever be accomplished either in yourselves or for mankind.

Each of you is to build a character which shall be the habitation of his spirit forever. You will bring something into its structure out of every relation in life. For that structure there can be but one sure foundation, and that is in a humble and unyielding faith in the personal Jesus Christ.

But these words of counsel need not be multiplied. All that has been said in the discourse has been intended for you. Remember that the great secrets of success in life are to be found only in faithfulness to God, in kindness to others, and in the strictest justice towards yourselves.

But what you propose to do in life, begin to do at once;

"The flighty purpose never is o'ertook,
Except the deed go with it."

One and another of your class has fallen by your side since your college days began. The remainder of life may be short for some of you, but its results will be eternal. Refuse, therefore, from this hour, no just task; neglect no known duty; fail not in your loyalty to God and His Christ,— and, be your days many or few, you will rear within yourselves characters strong, beautiful, and approved both of God and of men.

THE SEARCH FOR TRUTH.

Ever learning and never able to come to a knowledge of the truth.

2 TIMOTHY ii. 7.

BUT in this is there anything blameworthy or to be regretted? May it not be that the famous saying of Lessing is as applicable to moral and religious truth as to the truths of speculative philosophy? His words are "Did the Almighty, holding in His right hand 'Truth,' and in His left, 'Search after truth,' deign to proffer me the one I might prefer, in all humility, but without hesitation, I should ask for 'Search after truth.'" May it not be that a perpetual search after moral and religious truth would be better for man than the actual and assured possession of it? Let us see.

We doubtless delude ourselves when we think that with the acquisition of the objects of our pursuit we shall be able to sit down contented and at rest. We forget that every goal we reach becomes at once a starting point from which we hurry away in a race for another. Nothing acquired can, of itself, ever fill the mind with complete satisfaction. Every desire gratified becomes the parent of others; a want that is supplied to-day reveals others to-morrow, whose existence was before unsuspected.

There is reason, therefore, for the general statement that the pleasure of pursuit is greater than the pleasure of possession. The exhilaration of movement is more to be coveted than the repose of inactivity. And yet, movement unaccompanied by perception of stages of progress is not exhilarating, nor does it fail to become wearisome. The pleasure of movement is the pleasure of conscious progress; it is the satisfaction that springs from observing the rapidly-reached and passed goals that mark our advance towards the ultimate prize at which we aim. Grant that the pleasure of acquiring wealth, knowledge, or fame is greater than the pleasure of possessing these, yet this is true only because of the gratification that is felt in noticing the successive steps that take one onward towards the goal of his ambition. If there be disappointment at the final goal, it is because no other lies beyond it; the pleasure felt at each successive step was but a degree of the pleasure hoped for at the end.

But if pursuit be better than possession, why is it a matter of reproach that one should be ever learning and never able to come to a knowledge of the truth? The reason is plain. The reproach is not that one is ever learning the truth, and only progressively coming to a full knowledge of it,—this were commendable; but the reproach of the text was, that while certain persons were diligently learning about the truth, were giving their attention to subjects only accidentally or at best but incidentally connected with it, they were never able to come to a real and practical knowledge of the truth itself.

And indeed to be ever learning any subject and never coming to a real and definite knowledge of it, would be both discreditable and disquieting. To learn and never know is to fill the mind with weariness and disgust. In the practical affairs of life no state is more painful than that of uncertainty and doubt in matters where knowledge is possible, and where it must be had if failure is to be avoided. Even where to know is to be disappointed, knowledge is preferable to uncertainty. "It is a relief even to know the worst." And on the other hand, man is never more exultant than when conscious of a knowledge of what he has in hand.

Now all that has been thus said is doubly true of a knowledge of moral and religious truth. It is specially so of the satisfaction accompanying a knowledge of it. With every new acquisition in the pursuit of it comes a new joy. Over its accumulated stores the soul rejoices as it can over no other possessions. Wealth never satisfies except as a means to something higher and better than itself. Knowledge brings joy only because it opens windows through which we have wider views of the universe. Wealth also has its limits as a means; and knowledge of science, even the largest, is circumscribed in its power to satisfy. No amount of wealth can ever purchase character, or ever satisfy the yearnings of the heart; no degree of knowledge of things can ever fill the aching void of the moral nature. But the power of moral and religious truth is commensurate with every want of the soul. It alone can teach the right use of wealth; it alone can transform knowledge into true wisdom.

But here the question arises whether there can be any

certainty that the knowledge of such truth as we have been speaking of be attainable; whether the most careful search for it can ever take us, after all, beyond the region of mere probability. The question is a reasonable one. Let us see what answer can be given to it.

It must be admitted that our knowledge of some things in this world is exact, complete, and demonstrable. We know, for instance, that water is composed of the two simple elements, hydrogen and oxygen. We know this for absolute certainty, because we can resolve water into these elements, and again can combine the elements into water. We know also that within a single ray of white light lie all the colors of the rainbow. We know this, because out of the single ray we can educe all the colors of the rainbow, and all these colors we can gather and combine again into the single ray of white light. Thus far, our knowledge of water and light is assured. What light really is we never may be able absolutely to determine. What was the origin of water, or why it exists as water, we may never be able to say. And so of a thousand other things in nature which conceal from us their secrets, although our knowledge of their existence and of some of their properties is as definite and demonstrable as is the knowledge we have of our own existence. So much for our knowledge of the truths of nature.

Turn we now to moral and religious truth. And here shall we, like the Roman Governor Pilate, at the first sound of the word, turn on our heels and sneeringly ask: What is truth? or shall we, with the devotees of physical science, assume that nothing can ever be knowable to man which cannot be tested by the senses? If man be regarded as the creation of an omnipotent and omniscient Creator, is it reasonable to suppose him to have been tossed forth into a waste, howling wilderness of uncertainty, doubt, and despair, and not to have been endowed with the capacities, and surrounded with the sources of enlightenment, sufficient to give him some positive knowledge of his duties in life? Or, if we abandon the notion of a direct creation of man; if we regard the human intelligence, with all its powers and capacities, as the product of natural forces alone, is it credible that this intelligence should know the laws and truths of matter for certainty — laws that, at the closest, affect it but remotely — and never be able to certify to itself the laws and truths that immediately concern its own life and peace?

But here let us apply for a moment the scientific method in testing the trustworthiness of our knowledge of the truths of morality and religion. Let us see if our knowledge of these is less definite and assured than is our knowledge of the laws of physical science. Here is a human character; let us analyze it. We find it to be the product of certain fixed and well-known moral principles. These principles, put into practice, are just as sure to produce the type of character in which we have found them embodied, as hydrogen and oxygen, compounded in given quantities, are certain to give us water. Take the highest type of Christian character — gentle, pure, honest, patient, reverent, bold — and resolve every virtue composing it into the Christian truth, which each virtue embodies; and can there be any more doubt about the reality of those truths, or about the trustworthiness of our knowledge of them, or about the fact that all the truths are embodied in the New Testament idea of the person of Christ, than there is about the reality of the colors of the rainbow, or about the trustworthiness of our knowledge of these colors, or about the fact that the colors are all embodied in every ray of white light that falls from the heavens above us? A criticism that can see indubitable reality in the truths of physical science, and can find nothing but prudential maxims in the truths of morality, and nothing but fiction and fancy in the truths of religion, is not the criticism of real science nor of a sound philosophy.

But supposing the reality of religious truth to be admitted, and the trustworthiness of our knowledge of it to be established, the questions still recur, are there no obstacles that lie in the way of our search for it? Are there not conditions without which the search can never be conducted to a successful issue. Are there no tests by which the identity of truth may be determined when found? To these several questions let us, for a few minutes, give our attention.

And first as respects the obstacles. These, especially in our day, are not few nor slight, but they are chiefly in ourselves. And foremost among these is the existing and prevailing style of criticism. Sound criticism, let us never forget, is always in order. Human reason demands it. Christianity in all its teachings fosters it, challenging a scrutiny of its own claims, and by its injunctions prompting its adherents to look closely into the claims of whatever else is presented for their acceptance.

"Prove all things." "Believe not every spirit, but try the spirits." "Every one of us shall give account of himself to God." Christianity itself tried its own critical powers on the heathenisms it supplanted; and throughout the Christian centuries the more thoroughly men have entered into its spirit, the more careful they have been in their scrutiny of what was to be believed and what was to be practised. Nothing is more foreign to the spirit of the New Testament than the spirit of blind submission to hearsay, to tradition, to majority votes, or to ecclesiastical authority. It teaches every man to think, to inquire, to scrutinize, and then to decide for himself. Intelligent and sound criticism can trace its lineage directly to the New Testament Scriptures. But criticism, like everything else that is good, may be perverted. This, like many another offspring of Christianity, has been adopted by aliens, and so trained as to be turned against its parent.

Not a little of the criticism of moral and religious truth in our day is both unsound and unintelligent. Happily, much of the reckless criticism of the earlier historical records of Christianity, once so prevalent, is seen to have had no real foundation. And that kind of criticism, now in the ascendant, that accepts nothing as true which is not directly taught, or at least supported, by physical science, is a one-eyed and a one-legged criticism, that cannot be trusted to conduct us safely out of the wandering mazes of modern thought. Physical science is admirable in its own sphere; equally so are philosophy and religion in theirs. But the conclusions of one can never be safely taken as premises for the reasonings of the other; neither can the conclusions of one be justly used in combating the conclusions of the other. He who attempts to reason from the one to the other is as irrational as he who would attempt to travel by land and by water in one and the same vehicle.

The attempt, furthermore, to subject all moral and religious truth to the processes and conclusions of physical science is suicidal. The attempt can be made only by denying the trustworthiness of those elementary first truths which all minds accept and, of necessity, reason from. It can be made only by assuming that nothing can be trusted that cannot be subjected to the tests of the senses. But the assumption of certain first truths is common alike to religion and to all sciences, whether of mind, morals, or physics. Physical science assumes its own first truths and takes them along with it at every step of its progress. It talks of matter, and of force, and of physical laws, of atoms and molecules, and of space-filling ether, as of the most indubitable realities and truths; but on what ground, pray, except of the trustworthiness of the primary and necessary intuitions of the mind? But if the mind's necessary and intuitive recognition of force, and of law, and of atoms, or of whatever else is external to itself must be trusted, why repudiate its primary and necessary intuitions of what is internal and essential, and vital to its own existence and action? If our talk about matter, resting as it does on the intuitions of the mind, may be thus dogmatic and confident, why may not so much of our talk about morals and religion as rests on like intuitions, be equally confident? Does not the critic who objects to the intuitional basis of our moral and religious truth, like the foolish peasant in his reckless pruning, cut away the branch he sits on? In undertaking to undermine and blow up the citadel of religion, are not these critics involving themselves, as well as those whom they attack, in a common destruction?

Another obstacle in the way of our search for religious truth is the spirit of indifference. This is not an obstacle due to a passing fashion peculiar to our own time, but it is a chronic condition of human nature. It has two causes: the first, a pre-occupation of mind; the second, a low estimate of the worth of truth and of what it accomplishes for us. As to pre-occupation of mind, the provisions for our physical nature in this world are so profuse, they form so essential a part of the whole organization of society, they appeal to us so immediately, and minister so largely to present satisfaction, that before we are aware of it we are engrossed with the tangible, and indifferent to the invisible. We are too well pleased with what we have in hand, or can easily reach, to be anxious about what lies outside or beyond. As to the low estimate, the worth of what can be seen, and handled, and tasted, is easily appreciated. The advantage of material things in their hold on the attention of man is thus greatly preponderant over that of immaterial truth. The awards of the two also greatly differ. In material things, the connection between exertion and results is so close and outwardly apparent, that interest in pursuit never flags. The awards of moral and religious truth are in the character; they are inward, subtile, spiritual, and apparently remote. We walk by faith, and not by sight; and poor, weak human nature prefers that which can be easily grasped to that which can be had only by toiling and patiently waiting for it. But indifference, whatever its cause, never yet permitted any man to accomplish anything great or good in any pursuit, never allowed any one to work his way out of illusions into realities; in morals and religion, indifference is fatal as death.

Another obstacle with many, but not with all minds, is a positive dislike of religious truth; its exclusiveness is uncongenial to their tastes. It never flatters, never compromises, never stoops to expedients. It is intolerant of prejudice and of all error. Its method of dealing with whatever stands in its way is always short, sharp, and decisive. Its tone is always abrupt, and its demands explicit and unqualified. Entertained as a guest, it turns all other guests out of doors. It will be absolute master, or it will not tarry. And all this is extremely distasteful to the ease-loving and politic. To them truth is ill-natured and disagreeable; its society is, therefore, declined and its acquaintance ignored.

The truth, furthermore, refuses to be the guest of any one whose life is devoted to sensuality. It will keep no company with lust. Its scourge is always in its hand, ready to drive out from its presence every intruding passion. It will endure the presence of nothing "that defileth, or worketh abomination, or maketh a lie." To all evil-minded men the truth is unendurably repulsive. They hate it as did Ahab, the prophet, because it " never prophesieth good unto them but only evil."

Many dislike the truth also, because it is ever breaking the illusions of the present and throwing in upon them the light of the future. They dislike anticipation; they are afraid of what is to come; they hate the truth because it forces on their attention the connection of what is with that which is to be.

If, now, we be thus beset with difficulties in our search after truth, it is evident that we can come to a real knowledge of it only through the most painstaking care, and under conditions that cannot be slighted. Let us glance at these conditions for a moment.

The first that we will mention is a supreme regard for the truth, or preference for it to whatever else can be brought into comparison with it. Between it and our purpose to possess it, stand obstacles deeper and wider and higher than stand between us and any other object. Nothing can carry us triumphantly into its presence but a purpose supreme over every other. Our greatest calamity is that the obstacles are in ourselves and not in the truth, or in its surroundings; they are in our tastes and habits of mind, in our present and our pleasant self-delusions. Out from under the control of these and into the presence and possession of the real and true, nothing can take us but a desire that shall swallow up every other, a master passion that shall burn within us until it is transmuted into an energy that nothing can resist.

And why should not this be the one supreme passion of the soul? What possible end in life can be superior, can in any degree be compared with an assured knowledge of the truth? What are all other ends worth without that? What is life itself worth, if, while it lasts, it be a conscious and constant illusion; and when it ends, if it end in disappointment and despair? No! no! Let me know what is; let me know what I am; let me know what I stand on and am preparing for; let me know what I owe to my fellow-beings and what is due from me to the Eternal and Invisible One, and I can face life and its trials with composure; I can bend my back to its burdens with delight; I can fight the good fight of faith, knowing in what and in Whom I have believed, and assured that in the end all will be well. Surely no man is willing to be deceived in any earthly pursuit, and why should any be willing to be deceived in respect to what may come when earthly pursuits are ended?

A second requisite in coming to a knowledge of the truth is a prompt compliance with its exactions. These are not exorbitant, but they are unyielding. Truth, standing before the intellect as an abstraction, comes before the will as law clothed with awful authority. Thus it demands, first of all, instant obedience. If it comes to us, it will not be kept standing in the ante-room waiting our convenience. It will be taken at once into the inner court of the soul, or it will not enter. And it comes in the beginning, not like the summer sun in the fulness of its glory, but like a lantern shining in a dark place. And its faintest glimmer must be heeded, or it will not wax into a dawn; nor the dawn into the brightness of the day. If it throws its light outward on our pathway it will make plain to us but a single step at a time, and a step that must be taken or no second step will be revealed to us.

So also there must be an unconditional surrender of whatever is offensive to the truth. Prejudice and error and appetite and passion and the whole brood of evil spirits must be banished from the soul or truth will never become its guest. The chambers of the human soul are capacious enough to entertain the Infinite and Almighty One, but the demons of evil thoughts and evil passions congregating there make them into dens that are full of everything foul and loathsome. The eye of the soul, undimmed in its vision, can command a whole hemisphere of thought, but one small vice may shut the soul into blank darkness. Man also is endowed with the power of endless progress in his knowledge of truth; but one evil thought, microscopically small, may so eat into the marrow of his soul as to leave him forever crippled and in ignorance.

A third and the most essential requisite of all is an inward appreciation of the truth. Nor is this a requisite in morals and religion alone. Fitness to appreciate is equally indispensable to any kind of real knowledge. Nor does fitness to appreciate one kind qualify for an appreciation of another. One man may be incapable of following a mathematical demonstration, another of mastering a language, another of appreciating the finer qualities of style, another of discerning beauty in the skies, in a landscape, or in a work of art. To whatever kind of knowledge, therefore, we would invite the attention of any one, if we would not labor in vain, we must first of all see to it that he have the inward taste and capacity to perceive and understand.

Nor is it true that to require this condition is equivalent to requiring that one should already possess what it is proposed to impart to him. Surely the conditions for seeing an object are not the sight of it. The strength necessary to exertion is not itself the exertion. The eye, without which there can be no sight, certainly is not itself the sight. Neither is capacity to appreciate a given work of art to be confounded with actual knowledge of the work. The capacity for appreciation of art or of beauty in nature must doubtless be germinally within, or it never could be revealed nor cultivated, and the capacity must be in full exercise in every act of appreciation, and yet the capacity and the art are as distinct as the power and its exercise.

Nor, on the other hand, is there any good reason for affirming that, to require a right state of mind for acquiring a knowledge of the truth, is like begging the question in reasoning; that it requires a predisposition to accept what is congenial rather than what is absolutely true; that the truth found is in fact within us rather than without; in the language of the schools is subjective rather than objective. Let us see about this. One man has no taste for mathematics, and is incapable of understanding an intricate problem. To another the same problem is as clear as a sunbeam, and thrills him with delight. Are mathematics, therefore, unreal and the problem non-existent except in the mind of him who understands it and is pleased with it? An Indian chief is pleased with feathers and paint and a gay-colored blanket; a civilized man prefers a clean skin, a modest hat, and a neutral-colored coat. Do the feathers and paint and gay colored blanket exist only in the mind of the chief, and the hat and the coat only in the mind of the civilized? One man likes prose, another poetry; one is pleased with elaborate and brilliant rhetoric, another with simple and unadorned thought. Are the distinctions between prose and poetry, rhetorical ornament and baldness of thought, distinctions, therefore, existing only in the minds of those who are severally pleased with them? Nay; things are real, and the distinctions between things are realities. All truths are realities, and the truths of morality and religion are the most intensely real of all.

But there are distinctions among the requisites for different kinds of knowledge, and a difference in accountability for their absence. For some kinds of knowledge some men are helplessly disqualified. Incapacity for mathematics may be without remedy, color-blindness incurable. The perception of beauty, like the sense of humor and the gift of wit, may forever be denied to some natures. But the susceptibility for moral and religious truth is one and identical with human reason, and a relish for the truth, and a fitness to appreciate it, is always present where right reason is unhindered in its function. If wanting, it is because the eye of the soul has been darkened, because reason has been perverted in its function, and the moral affections have been corrupted. And if wanting it can be created; if lost it can be regained. If we do not like the truth it is because we are false to ourselves; because we are willing to be deceived; because we have been willing to sell our birthright for what is paltry and worthless and self-destroying.

If now moral and religious truth really exist, if under given conditions it may be made our own, the final question recurs: Are there any sufficient tests by which I can be assured that I have found it? Let us glance at one or two of these.

First of all, truth humbles one in his own eyes. It is always luminous, and light makes manifest, and there is nothing that so humbles a man in his own estimation as to see himself as he really is. But if what we regard as truth fills us with self-conceit and pride and contempt for others, it is manifestly error and not truth which we have embraced. It has been justly said that when Paul was a Pharisee he thought he was blameless; but when he became a Christian, he accounted himself the chief of sinners. The light of truth, like the presence of Deity, fills us with awe. He who sees it cries out with Job: "I have heard of thee by the hearing of the ear; but now mine eye seeth thee. Wherefore I abhor myself and repent in dust and ashes."

Again, truth is self-witnessing; it brings with it its own credentials; its very presence and power certify to its identity; it is fitted to the soul of man, and the soul of man is fitted to it. They are so fitted, not because either one was made for the other, but because they are counterparts of each other. Truth is the soul's mirror, revealing it to itself, revealing its capacities, its necessities, its duties, its destination. It is a mirror, because it is the soul's better self confronting the actual self. It is the truth, because it is a revelation of realities, laying bare what is, and so proclaiming what must be.

Again, truth is content with no single achievement, never stops with the fulfilment of its minor offices. It attacks not single errors, but all error; is never satisfied with mere pruning of vices, but lays the axe at the root of all vice. It seats itself at once in the centre of the soul, and begins a reconstruction of the whole being. Implacable, it spares no evil; impartial, it leaves no part of our nature uncontrolled. It is never content with single virtues, but demands all virtue. It will tolerate no dwarfed or one-sided character, but demands a completed symmetry. Its command is: " Whatsoever things are true, whatsoever things are honest, whatsoever things are just, whatsoever things are pure, whatsoever things are lovely, whatsoever things are of good report; if there be any virtue, and if there be anything praiseworthy, think on these things." "And besides this, giving all diligence, add to your faith, virtue; and to virtue, knowledge; and to knowledge, patience; and to patience, godliness; and to godliness, brotherly-kindness; and to brotherly-kindness, charity." Truth builds a character that is composed of every virtue, and crowns it with a charity that never fails.

Need I remind this audience that the truth we have thus described once dwelt on earth in human form? That the truth thus incarnate, though in humblest guise to the common eye, was yet, to the eye that could see and the ear that could hear, clothed with the majesty and spoke with the authority of Godhead. "To this end was I born," said Jesus, "and for this cause came I into the world, that I should bear witness to the truth. I am the Way, the Truth, and the Life. Every one that is of the truth heareth my voice." He who thus lived and spoke eighteen hundred years ago, lives and speaks to us to-day. Shall we spend our days in learning and un-learning, in questioning and guessing and doubting and hoping and fearing, when it is so easy once for all to find our way into the presence of Him who, for us and for all men, is the Truth now and forever? Amen!

Gentlemen of the Graduating Class: Four years of your lives have been spent in associated study. That association is now to be broken up. Under such guidance as has been given you, you have been working in various departments of knowledge. That you should have learned nothing in all these years is incredible. It is not too much, perhaps, to suppose that from the time of your coming together you have every day been learning something. How much of this has been worthless — how much may need in the future to be unlearned — it is needless now to inquire. Something, doubtless, has been learned that will abide with you till all knowledge shall vanish away in the presence of the uncreated Light.

But the one question I wish to invite you each to answer in the secret of his own heart to-day is this: In all these years of your college life, ever learning as you have been, have you come any nearer than you were at the outset to that knowledge of the eternal verities, the truths of God, the truth as it is in Jesus, without which all other knowledge will prove in the end to be worthless, and possibly a delusion and a snare? All knowledge and all truth are but parts of an infinite whole; links of continuous chains, so that strike whatever link you may, tenth or ten thousandth, you strike a chain that, followed up, will bring you to the very throne of eternal truth. If hitherto you have rested only in the passing present, is not this the day in which you should begin to look seriously into the significancy of life? The present never stays. Nothing earthly abides. Self, truth, and God alone abide everlastingly the same. With truth and God on your side, eternal peace is yours; with truth and God against you, endless unrest and despair.

The war between truth and error is fiercer to-day than ever before. Of this war you cannot, if you would, be idle spectators. On the one side or the other, by the very necessities of your nature, you must be combatants. Bids for your enlistment on one side will be loud, numerous, persistent, and boastful; on the other you will hear, in tones that are low and slow, but articulate and distinct, the words: "Fight the good fight; be thou faithful unto death, and I will give thee a crown of life." What were the whole world worth to you should you purchase it at the cost of a single truth. Better that you were now and here blotted out of existence, than that you should live slaves to your own senses and die at the last despicable in your own eyes and in the eyes of God and of all good men.

Often in the fight for the just, the good, and the true, you will find yourselves under sunless and starless heavens. Black clouds will hang loweringly above you, but remember that they are clouds,

"whose nether face
To grovelling mortals frowns and darkens all,
But on whose billowy backs, from man concealed,
The glaring sunbeams play."

Let not your faith in God forsake you, and in due time the Sun of Righteousness shall shine upon you with healing in His beams.

If your fight in life is to be for the right, the real, and the true, strike your first blow for it to-day. To-morrow is not yours; it never may be. Once and again, in your college days, you have heard the lesson: "Whatsoever thy hand findeth to do, do it with thy might; for there is no work, nor device, nor knowledge, nor wisdom, in the grave, whither thou goest." A classmate dropped from your ranks in death; his work was done, his warfare ended. A revered and much loved teacher, in the fulness of his strength, in the prime of his powers, fell battling for the truth. Of life nothing is certain but its end and its awards. Sure only of these, let us stand undismayed each in his lot.

> "Solemn before us
> Veiled, the dark portal,
> Goal of all mortal;
> Stars silent o'er us,
> Graves under us silent,
> But heard are the voices,
> Voice of the Sages,
> The worlds and the ages;
> 'Choose well, your choice is
> Brief and yet endless.'"

THE SURE VICTORY OF FAITH.

Who is he that overcometh the world but he that believeth that Jesus is the Son of God?
1 JOHN v. 5.

NO human life was ever worthily lived that was not also a life of struggle and conflict. No kind of life, from the lowest vegetive to the highest spiritual, can maintain its existence except by resistance to forces that, unresisted, would sooner or later extinguish it. The vital germ of the seed must struggle against the rainfall that threatens to drown it, against the cold of night that threatens to freeze it, and against the heat of day that threatens to scorch it. Animal life can preserve itself only by incessant struggle with forces that, left to themselves, would destroy it. And what is true of the natural life is equally true of the intellectual and the moral; these cannot live except by struggles with obstacles that would shut them into darkness and death.

And by a universal law of compensation, it so happens that the very struggles necessary to the maintenance of any species of life are the very means by which alone the fulness of the life is attainable. Vicissitude of storm and calm, of cloud and sunshine, of cold and heat invigorate the plant. Battling with the forces of nature develops sinew and muscle, and gives health of nerve. Grappling with the problems of science and the great truths of philosophy ministers strength to the intellect. The moral life of the soul becomes robust and healthy only through endurance of trials and victory over temptations.

There is a profound philosophy in the injunction: "Count it all joy when ye fall into divers temptations."

And every kind of natural life is endowed with an inherent power to fight its own way in the world. The light-winged seed that floats in the evening air drops into the rich mould of a cleft of the rock, shoots downward its delicate rootlets into the narrow depths, and upward its tender stem into the inviting air; the tender stem becomes the huge trunk with outspreading branches, and the delicate rootlets the giant roots that crowd asunder the oppressive rocks. The tilted slab of the sidewalk, beneath which runs the root of the shade-tree, proclaims the presence of a life power that can push its own way in spite of obstructions. The infant intellect, surrounded by objects that rouse it to thought, waxes into an energy that refuses to be stayed by any barrier. But the moral life of the soul, weak from its birth, and enfeebled by the pestilent atmosphere of what the Scriptures call "the world," must have divine help, or it sickens and dies.

"The world" is human society actuated by principles that exclude all regard for the character and will of the Supreme Being. It denotes a spirit and a policy that find all motives to action in the life that now is. It includes, also, all the forces of evil that rule in human nature. The lust of the flesh, the lust of the eyes, and the pride of life are but constituent parts of it. The Scriptures know nothing of the triad, "the world, the flesh, and the devil." The flesh is one of the forces of the world, and the devil is its prince and ruler. Whatever alienates man from God and sets up self-indulgence instead of self-subjection to the rule of the true and the good, is the world, and is inimical to man. And worldliness, whatever its outward aspect, is always the spirit that sets up self as the object of its supreme regard.

Nor is the world, as thus described, a religious chimera, a bugbear of pietists, an imaginary maelstrom in the sea of life, laid down on its chart by men who have never explored it. Neither is the world an extinct monster, that may have existed when the apostles wrote the New Testament Scriptures, but has now vanished before the advancing light of science and religion. It never was more real, nor more active, nor more deceptive, nor more remorseless or pitiless than it is to-day. But it has no unchanging form. It is not a mode, but a spirit and a power. It is many visaged. It can wear the livery of heaven; it can diffuse around itself the very atmosphere of paradise. Undiscerning people often denounce that as worldly which is only seemingly so, and applaud that as Christian which is only worldliness with a visor on.

Two mistakes are here to be carefully guarded against. The one is that of the narrow-minded zealot who mistakes the appearance of worldliness for its reality. To him the worldling is he who possesses, and not he whose heart is eaten out by the cankering desire to possess. He forgets that the world is not in one's possessions, but in setting the heart on them, and in a weak and foolish misuse of them. It is not in the flesh, but in the lusts of it; not in the eyes or in objects that are pleasing to the sight, but in that eating desire that works through the eye for self-gratification; it is not in the means of luxurious indulgence, but in the silly vanity, the pride of life that flaunts the means and the indulgence as objects of admiration. There may be incomparably more of the world beneath calico and gilt jewelry, than beneath velvet and laces and diamonds. The decorated lackey who flaunts the livery may be a genuine worldling as compared with the quiet soul that sits within his mansion, filled with thoughts of sweet charities and consecrated purposes.

The other mistake is that of the over-liberal, who believe that the world, in its traditional Christian sense, is now an empty word and nothing more. If it once denoted a dangerous reality, that reality has now ceased to exist. To talk of it as something real, is to indulge in idle cant. In their estimation the world has become so far humanized, if not Christianized, as to be no longer at enmity with God. It is a part of the creation of God, and as such is to be rejoiced in. They, too, like the zealot, err in judging only by the outward appearance. The world has indeed been taught to put on a less repulsive attire; its tones have been softened; its features are less gross; its deformities are veiled; its vices are hidden from public gaze; it even puts on an air of refinement and culture. But it is the same old enemy of the apostolic days, however changed in tone and outward appearance. So long as it shuts out the will of God from its motives, so long as it panders to self and self-indulgence, so long as it fails to make the character of Christ the ideal type of humanity, so long it will remain the enemy of God and man.

Now with the spirit of this world which is everywhere around us, insinuating and seductive, every one of us must fight and overcome it, or it will overcome us. And it can be conquered by no weapons of its own kind. "I trample on Plato's pride," sneered Diogenes, while treading with his dirty sandals on Plato's purple couch. "Yes," said Plato, "but with a greater pride." No back fire can arrest and defeat its course. We never can overcome it by a bribery of one or more of its forces to join us in fighting against the others. We never can —

> "Compound for sins we are inclined to
> By damning those we have no mind to."

No league with the lust of the eyes can vanquish the lust of the flesh. No alliance with the pride of life can overcome either the lust of the flesh or the lust of the eyes. Every principle of the world is vital with the spirit of every other. Not one of them but in the end will turn traitor, and betray us into the hands of all the others. Victory can come to us from only one source and by one method, — from Jesus Christ, who was born into the world to overcome it; and from a thorough faith in Him as One who overcame and is now seated at the right hand of God.

But let us not mistake as to what it is that is to give us the victory. It is not a mere assent to the dogma of the incarnation. Multitudes of men had mastered the world before Jesus was born into it. Moses and the prophets all triumphed over it. And it was their faith in God founded on such knowledge as they had of Him, which gave them the victory. Moses, seeing dimly and from afar, and believing in what he saw, fought the world in Egypt, and laid the foundations of a new religion and a new civilization. The prophets, with clearer vision and stronger faith than were vouchsafed to Moses, continued the warfare, lifting religion and civilization to a yet higher plane. Faith in the still clearer teachings of Jesus as the Son of God can do for us to-day more than it ever did for Moses or any prophet. He who now masters the world will believe in Jesus as speaking by the authority of God, and in His teachings, as being God's latest and most authentic communications to man. To what some of these teachings are, and the connection of our faith in them with the victory of which we are speaking, let us for a moment turn our attention.

1. Jesus taught the minute fatherly care of God for every human being. He was not, as some have affirmed, the first to teach God's fatherhood of our race. This had been plainly taught by the prophets centuries before Jesus was born. It was evidently a common idea in the time of Malachi, four hundred years before the birth of Jesus. Even the Romans were accustomed to speak of Jupiter as father of gods and men. But Jesus, as no Gentile or Jew ever could, brought God home to the human soul as the always present and always gracious Father, whose infinite eye nothing is too minute to escape, and whose infinite pity nothing human is too insignificant to move. Every event of life is foreseen; every want of the soul an object of His care. To every human being is assigned his position in life, his duties and his trials, the measure of his abilities and the number of his days. Infinite Power and Infinite Love,

according to Jesus, are both busily active in providing for the wants of the human soul.

Now, where faith in the teaching of Jesus makes this truth to become a practical reality, there the power of the world is broken. Where there is a sense of God's presence, there the world is vanquished. The spirit of the world will flee from His presence like a demon of darkness. He who clearly reads the will of God in each event and duty of life, who distinctly hears the voice of the Most High saying, this is the way, walk ye in it; whose one prayer is, Thy will, not mine, be done, will be one of the sons of God, whatever his earthly estate and whatever his personal endowments. No earthly incident can detract from the dignity of his character or disturb the serenity of his mind. Poverty will not dishearten nor riches inflate; opprobrium will not daunt nor flattery delude; neglect will not sour nor applause make vain. Engrossed by the highest thoughts that can engage the mind, and filled with the purest content the soul can know, the illusions of the world can no more move him, than the noonday shadows that flit along the mountain side can shake its rocky strength.

Nor is this faith which conquers, a mere affectation of belief, a kind of forced credulity to keep one's courage up amid the uncertainties of life. It knows on what it builds. And when physical science comes to it, and prates of earthly events as the product of physical laws with which no Deity can intermeddle, it remembers that no science or philosophy ever yet reached its conclusions that did not force on the mind the inquiries whence and whither; inquiries to which the answers of Jesus were explicit; answers that give to every one who will receive them the victory and the rest that all men crave.

2. Again, the teachings of Jesus are distinctively ethical. He did not propound a religion on which morality was to be grafted as one of its products, but the fulfilment of moral law was the one all-inclusive object for which He came into the world, and for which His religion was established. Of that object He never for an instant, in word or deed, lost sight. The result was that He gave an exhaustive exposition of moral law for all nations and for all time. Multitudes of men have set up for ethical teachers, but not one iota of moral truth have they added to His teachings; not one ethical principle taught by Him have they invalidated. The one distinguishing characteristic of His religion among all the religions the world has yet known, is its unyielding regard for moral law, for moral conduct, and for moral character. All moral laws are embodied in it, all are enforced by it, and to every one who will receive it, all are fulfilled by it.

Now the moral laws to which Christianity is thus devoted are not repealable enactments. Indeed, they are not enactments at all. They are simple declarations of what is, and eternally must be; they are the essential principles of all rational existences. Their seat is in the eternal nature of God, and they are the constitutive principles of every rational creature of God. They hold together the universe of rational intelligences, just as the law of gravitation holds together the universe of matter. They can no more be repealed than the law of gravitation can be annihilated. Heaven and earth shall pass away, but not one jot or tittle of them shall fail. And man can no more escape them than he can escape from himself.

The moral laws of its being also bring the soul into direct and conscious relation to its Maker and Lawgiver. They are to the eye of the soul in respect to the nature of God what the stars are to us on a cloudless night in respect to the celestial spaces; they light up for us the infinite depths of the divine nature, filling the soul with emotions that almost strike it dumb with amazement. They bring the soul into the very presence-chamber of the Almighty; they are His articulate voice to man. No wonder that in the presence of these laws the conscience should wield a power that entitles it to be called the vicegerent of the Almighty. In the heart where faith in Jesus gives to law and conscience this rightful rule, can the world hold sway?

3. Again the religion of Jesus assures us of the presence in the soul of a divine and indwelling Helper. Other religions have restricted the divine presence to particular localities. They have made the divine favor to be specially procured by sacrifices in given temples and by pilgrimages to specific shrines. Jesus taught that true spiritual worship, wherever offered, is acceptable to God; that the real shrine at which divine blessings are dispensed is in the heart of the worshipper. It is in the heart that He has established His kingdom, and it is there, before the eye of the soul, that He is transfigured to His disciples. To them He has pledged Himself to be present to the end of the world, and to sustain to them the most intimate conceivable of rela-

tions. "I am the vine, ye are the branches; without me ye can do nothing."

Precisely what the nature of this relation of Christ with His disciples may be, it is useless here to say. If we reject, on the one hand, the notion of a mystical union of persons, still more, on the other, would we repudiate the notion of a mere moral influence of thought. Christianity is not a mere system of moral-religious philosophy that, emanating from Jesus, has contrived to survive the waste of centuries. Socrates started such a system, and all that in reality now survives of it is his name applied to a method of instruction. The Platonic philosophy, unfolded with all the aid of the highest rhetorical art, is to-day the study and admiration of a cultured few, but it never shaped the destiny of a single people or moulded the character of a single generation. Christianity, on the other hand, beginning in the humblest possible guise with Jesus of Nazareth, has transformed nations, has moulded the character of untold generations, and to-day has raised the foremost peoples of earth to a higher plane and a purer air than the race has ever known before.

Evidently the power that has wrought all this is not an idle tradition. The Christian Church, through which the change has been wrought, is not a monument to an empty name, is not an association of people held together by ringing endless changes on the words and deeds of One who lived and passed away like other men, but of One who died and rose again, and to-day is the personal Source of a life-giving energy. The Christian Church, with all its multitudinous names and sub-divisions, is but a single body organized by the Holy Ghost around the one glorified Christ. To be born into this Christian Church by a true spiritual birth is to come into direct personal relation to this one personal Christ as a living and a life-giving Person.

The Christianity that to-day is to give victory and personal freedom to believers in it, must be, not a philosophy, nor a theosophy, nor a creed, nor a special form of worship, nor a church, but a life and a power, — a life emanating from the divine-human Person who was its original source, and flowing into the hearts of men through that living faith which itself is victory.

But here we do not forget that there have been eminent men, men of large knowledge, of high character and of brilliant parts, who have not avowed themselves to be practical believers in Jesus. But their eminence, and learning, and character, and brilliancy have not been because of their unbelief. Neither is there any evidence that belief might not have added to the grounds of their distinction. The religion of Jesus is not repressive; mankind have not gone backward since receiving it. It is to-day the patron and nurse of all sound learning. Was Faraday any less eminent and skilful as a chemist for being a devout and earnest Christian? Would his eminent successor be any less entitled to distinction had he been like his eminent master, an earnest believer in Jesus?

Two very noted men, whose praises are on the lips of nations, have lately gone to their final accounts, neither of whom was accounted a believer. Both were pre-eminently students and lovers of nature. One studied nature in all the thousand attitudes and processes through which the numberless forms of life that lie around us have come into being. He studied closely and minutely the successive steps by which the ever-lengthening and ever-widening procession of life has spread itself over the earth. He never ventured to deny that behind the successive steps was a life-giving agency that vitalized all the boundless mechanism. This has been reserved for the sciolists, who know so much more than the scientists. Here, as always, " Fools rush in where angels fear to tread."

The other great student of nature turned all his thoughts to the study of man, as presented in history and in human society. To his eye, nature presented herself not as a succession of mechanical forces, but of volitional energies. He was no scientist, but a cool and sometimes cynical critic, the Montaigne of the nineteenth century. He neither affirmed nor denied the existence and the presence among men of a personal God; he was not a practical believer in the divine messages of Jesus. And he neither himself, in the best sense, mastered the world, nor do his writings so lift men out of themselves above the spirit of worldliness as to inspire them with a desire to become benefactors of their race. Can any one believe that had Darwin and Emerson been avowed and earnest believers in Jesus, they need have been any less eminent than they were, or any less useful in the labors to which they devoted themselves?

Gentlemen of the Graduating Class: Could each of you, gifted at this moment with foresight, trace the pathway of his life up to the point or moment of its ending, the sight would doubtless fill you with emotions which no language can describe. To some one of you there would perhaps be presented only a few faint footsteps, leading nowhere and ending within sight of its beginning. To another it might be a path too devious for the eye to follow, and terminating in gloom and disappointment. To another, a common highway where thousands travel, an undistinguishable crowd. To another, a narrow path among thorns and thistles, and through narrow defiles, but ending in sunshine and triumph. To another, it would be a lengthened pathway "o'er moor and fen, o'er crag and torrent," through wide vales and across distant hills, and ending afar off amid the golden light of the sinking sun. Happily, a merciful Providence has hidden all with a veil which you can neither lift nor pierce. But from behind the veil an Almighty hand is stretched out, if you will but take it, that shall guide you in safety. It shall turn your failures into successes, your disappointments into fulfilment of better hopes, and your defeats into triumphs. To every one of you there is also, if you will but apply to it, a secret store of armament for every emergency. If you will, you can,—

"from that secret store,
Work linked armor for your souls before
They shall go forth to war among mankind."

Thus armed, your victory will be sure. That you may be thus armed, first settle it in your minds that whatever your career is to be, long or short, troublous or peaceful, attended with the applause or with the hisses of men, it shall be, so far as you can understand, precisely that which God has marked out for you. There is an allotted work for each of you, and inquiry will reveal it. Ascertaining it, devote yourselves to it with all the energy, patience, and industry of an undivided nature. The resources of the universe will be at your service when once you are at your appointed tasks. Come what may, the life of every one of you will be a success, if but from the heart there shall rise the daily prayer, "Thy will, not mine, be done." The prince of this world, coming to you with the offer of a kingdom for your service, will flee from you as from one who has power to overcome both him and his kingdoms. And this is a victory that is alike possible for every one of you. Never forget that the reward for a right use of one talent is every whit as large in proportion as that for a right use of ten. "To him that overcometh will I grant to sit with me on my throne, even as I also overcame and am set down with my Father on His Throne."

Let me, also, here remind you that, related to the Eternal Being as you are, you cannot, if you would, escape either His power or His presence. The laws of His moral nature are also equally the laws of yours. You are bound to His throne by bonds which can never be severed. With these laws you can refuse to comply, but the refusal will react with penalties which no tears can annul. Of these laws Jesus was the one expounder for all time. To His expositions your hearts respond as the stringed instrument to the touch of a master. He makes the articulate voice of God to speak within you, saying: "This do and thou shalt live." Believe, then, in this Jesus as one who is able to teach, to guide, and to save you; and you shall know what it is to be crowned at the last as victors in the battle of life.

And, finally, let me remind you of the way in which this same Jesus will aid you in the battle. Though it be an inward strife in which no human helping can avail, it yet is a strife in which your own unaided strength will never suffice. No sense of obligation, no knowledge of law, no voice of conscience, no moral influence of truth, can minister that special strength without which victory never can be yours. The spirit of evil, the spirit of this world that surrounds us like an atmosphere, pervading society, and penetrating to the very foundations of life, can never be expelled from within, except through the presence and aid in the soul of the personal Spirit that helps our infirmities. Thus aided, you cannot fail. Trusting in your own strength, defeat will be inevitable. You —

> "can make your youth
> The sepulchre of hope, where evil thoughts
> Shall grow like weeds on a neglected tomb;"

or you can make it as a garden of the Lord, wherein, in due time, "a harvest of high hopes and noble enterprises" will be sure to be gathered. Which of these it shall be is for you to decide. Deciding rightly, there stands for you all the never-changing promise: "Be thou faithful unto death, and I will give thee a crown of life."

PERILS OF THE PRESENT DAY.

Save yourselves from this untoward generation.

Acts ii. 40.

IT certainly is from no disposition to reflect on the present generation as evil above all that have preceded it, that these words have been selected as a text. Every generation is attended with its own dangers, against which every individual of it needs to be always on his guard. The dangers of our day differ from those of other times chiefly in their number and in the false guises under which they present themselves. They stand before us under the names and claims of being manifest marks of progress, as being the stages of advance beyond all that have preceded us, for which intelligent people should be glad and give thanks. Some of our greatest perils lie in these boasted advances.

There are two primary sources and one secondary, from which the moral and religious dangers of all times have commonly arisen. The first source is in the arrest and decay of religious thought; the second is in the reckless haste and confusion always attendant on revolutions in religious thinking, and the third in the erratic action of human impulse and passion, which is sure to reveal itself when the restraints of religion are slackened, as they never fail to be in times of religious revolution. No one of the three ever exists in total separation from the others. The first never fails in due time to introduce the second, and the second is never unattended by the third. All are commonly in full force at one and the same time. Let me explain.

All life, in the simplest definition of it, is movement. And that life is fullest and strongest which has just momentum enough to convert whatever obstacle it encounters into means for its own development; and its development is always through an ever-recurring series of stages or types. In vegetable life, the germ that shoots up, buds, blossoms, and fruits, has no sooner imparted the life that is in it to the seed by which that life is to be perpetuated, than itself falls to the earth and disappears. And as with the forms of vegetable life, so, also, with the forms of intellectual and moral and religious life. As with philosophy, so, also, with religion. Throughout the changing centuries have been the ever-recurring changes in types of thought and modes of activity. The types and forms that sufficed for Abraham were inadequate to the times of Moses. What was full of meaning to Moses became barred and unprofitable to Isaiah, and was old and ready to vanish away with the Apostle Paul. The formularies framed in the early centuries from the writings of the apostles, vital as they were in every part, became, in due time, limp and flabby, requiring new statements, and these restatements requiring the modifications and remodifications made necessary by the changing currents of the changing centuries. The Council of Nice would have started to its feet in dismay and indignation to have heard the decrees of the Council of Trent, and the Council of Trent would have shouted its anathemas at the Council of our day at Rome that ventured to decree the infallibility of the Pope. Every new epoch has required new statements and a recasting of the phraseology, in which it will express even the oldest and most fundamental of beliefs.

It is strictly in line, therefore, with the experience of all preceding times, that the Protestant formularies of the sixteenth and seventeenth centuries should now be subject to criticism, which, in the estimation of not a few of the existing generation, greatly invalidate their authority. Some of the dogmatic teachings of these formularies founded on literal interpretations of Scripture metaphors, can no longer be vindicated by any just principles of interpretation. Their conceptions also of the origin and inspiration of the Scriptures have slowly and silently given place to other and different views. Thus, from the traditions and creeds of Christendom, it is evident that some of the meanings originally conveyed by them have gradually slipped away. The original meanings having vanished, the words in which the meanings were expressed are falling into disuse and decay.

On the one hand, alarmed by this decay the indolent and unreflecting rashly infer that the life of Christianity itself is dying out; that, as a religion, it may not be divine in its authority, and so they will trouble themselves no more about its teachings. On the other hand, emboldened by the changed meanings and waning authority of the creeds, and by an abandonment of the doctrine of the inspired authority of the Scriptures, the restlessly inquisitive and self-confident are boldly pushing forward a revolution in religious thought that, like all other revolutions, threatens a devastation and ruin which the movers of it can never repair. In this revolution is a second source of danger. Swept by it from their footing the adventurous, as well as the evil-minded and evil-disposed, are rushing madly and blindly into a blank disbelief in all revealed religion.

The restraints of religion thus loosened by the apathy of indifference on the one hand, and by the noisy pretensions of scepticism on the other, there is opened a third source of danger in the multitudinous perversions, deficiencies, and excesses into which a world of solicitations to our senses is ever alluring us.

Let us look at some of the special evils springing from these several sources, from which we need to strive diligently to save ourselves.

First among these dangers is a fixed habit of doubt and a settled disbelief in all positive religion. Doubt, as a withholding of assent till the grounds for yielding it are clearly understood and accepted, is always a sign of health, both intellectual and moral. Blind assent is credulity, and credulity always makes an easy prey to error. Credulity invites imposture, which never fails to appear. But the habit of doubt works mischief of another kind; it puts an arrest on all the natural activities of the soul. Doubt fights no battles, achieves no victories, overcomes no obstacles, bridges no chasms, builds no highways of thought and action across the deserts and bogs of life, but stands and waits till, recoiling on itself, it deadens every energy of the soul. Its chief peril is, that by an invariable law it grows, sooner or later, into settled distrust, and from distrust waxes into unbelief, and from unbelief into disbelief in everything and everybody but self.

An explicit and avowed disbelief in the claims of all supernatural religion is not so uncommon in our day as it once was. And no wonder that it should be so. The apostles of unbelief are propagating their dogmas with a zeal and confidence born of something else than doubt. To break down our confidence in the supernatural, and thus to destroy that faith in God which it inspires, has been declared by them to be a work of benevolence to man. To expel the thought of God from the minds of men, to drive out the living Christ from the hearts of men, and to extinguish the hopes which Christ inspires, is the work of beneficence in which these apostles of a new gospel are avowedly engaged. It is the benevolence of him who, having no shelter of his own, is intent on destroying that of every one else; of him who, because he is himself blind, insists that everybody else would be greatly improved if only his eyes could be put out.

And what do the heralds of unbelief propose as a substitute for Christian faith? Surely they are not insane enough to suppose that any human being can live without some kind of faith, faith in something or somebody. Will it be any more refining and exalting to man to be persuaded that when he looks into the face of nature, he can see in it nothing but blank matter, moved only by purposeless force, bearing no trace of a personal will, and wisdom, and love? Will it be any more inspiring and invigorating to the energies and affections of men to listen to the voices of nature, and hear in them no articulate tones of paternal care and sympathy, but only the ceaseless clangor and rattle and roar of mechanical forces? Will it give us any higher type of humanity to believe that we live in a Godless world, and not under the eye of Infinite Compassion and Love? Will faith in an impersonal force, rather than in an infinite Father of Spirits give us a man of purer affections, of nobler aspirations, of more genuine moral heroism, of more complete self-devotion to the common weal?

Nay, but surely no intelligent preacher of unbelief would rob the soul of any ethical restraints or of any just motive to ethical achievement. No; but it is ethics alone that they propose to put in the place of religion. And whence have they derived the ethics with which they propose to supplant Christianity? Is there one solitary moral principle which they find to be necessary, and which themselves have discovered, to complete the teachings of Jesus? Is there one of the moral precepts of Christianity which they have found to have worked mischief to mankind? Are they not appropriating bodily the ethics of Christianity while repudiating the religion which propounded them, and which alone can give them efficiency?

Unbelief has undertaken an impossible task. It begins by doing violence to some of the first and strongest instincts of the personal being. It assures man that there is no archetypal Father for whom, like a lost child in the dark, he instinctively yearns and calls; that the future is only an eternal silence which no sound can break; that outside of the life that now is, only infinite nothingness awaits us. And with such teaching can any rational mind expect long to be content?

A second peril, growing out of the one just dwelt upon, is the temptation to an unnatural divorce of religion and morality. In attempted counteraction of the tendency to doubt and unbelief, religion is too often so presented as to throw morality into the background as of secondary importance. Against this danger not a single subdivision of the Christendom of to-day is keeping itself strictly on its guard; Romanists and Protestants alike are prone to fall into it. And for this there has been a common cause. All alike have sought to strengthen the faith of men in the Gospel of Christ as a divine revelation. Just in proportion as they have sought to revive a drooping faith, they have quickened the religious emotions. Religion, even when its faith has been most vital and active, was never more emotional than it is to-day. And this is true whether the religion be that of Sacerdotalism, of Liberalism, or of Evangelicalism. Sacerdotalists make the Church the ark of safety within which the believer is to seat himself and rejoice. Liberalists make the individual consciousness the Shekinah of the Almighty, before which each is to bow in joyous adoration; and Evangelicals, resting all on the vicariousness of Christ and His work, too often content themselves with the joy of singing the refrain: —

> "Nothing great or small
> Remains for me to do;
> Jesus died and paid it all,
> Yes, all the debt I owe."

Thus one of the dangers common to every form of religion in our time is a disposition to rest in the blessedness of its hopes, rather than to bear the burden of its duties; to enjoy the luxury of its emotions, rather than to toil in the cultivation of its virtues; to be grateful for the gratuitousness of its provisions, rather than to submit to its requirements and to become fit for its blessings.

But, on the other hand, there are those who insist on attempting to realize all morality without the aid of religion; who refuse to recognize any divine authority in the Christian religion and denounce the dogmas of the Church as immoral in their influence. And it must be admitted that, so far as the letter of moral law is concerned, their morality may be real and praiseworthy. But it is the morality of the outer man, and not of the inner. It is a body without a soul. As the emotions of the mere religionist will vanish in worship, in song, and empty words of prayer, unless embodied in deeds, so a morality unquickened by love to the Supreme One as the all-loving Father, and to the Son, who is both the Father's Revealer and Reconciler, is a morality that, like Jonah's gourd, will wither at the first touch of the worm of selfishness that lies at the heart of it. A morality which is to abide must be rooted alike in the convictions of the intellect and in the affections of the heart.

The world has had in it an abundance of immoral religions and of irreligious moralities, but that the religion of Jesus Christ, every principle of which inculcates and, properly applied, begets both the soul and the body of morality, should be degraded into a mere instrument for the creation of transient emotions, is an offence to

Heaven and a crime against humanity; and that any one, appropriating the ethics of Christianity should attempt out of these to create a morality in repudiation of the religion in which alone the ethics are grounded and can be made vital, is to be guilty of impiety and of the folly of expecting grain without soil, and trees without roots.

> "What comes from heaven to heaven by nature clings,
> And, if dissevered thence, its course is short."

But again, thirdly, when unbelief prevails, when religion fails of morality, and morality affects to repudiate religion, then spring forth into activity all those principles of our nature which, though natural and instinctive in themselves, work endless mischief when unchecked by the restraints of religion.

First among these is an inordinate coveting of large possessions. The desire of gain is a universal human instinct, — an instinct as active in the breast of the savage as in that of the civilized man. And properly controlled, it is one of the most useful of human instincts. It is the first moving force in the work of civilization. To be a personal being is to desire the completest being; to live by the chase is to desire the amplest supply of implements for success in the chase; to live in the midst of the appliances of civilization is to seek to possess as many of the best of these as may lie within our reach. But the impulse to acquire, like every other instinct, yielded to and uncontrolled, speedily waxes into a passion that will subordinate, if it can, every other to its service. Like a vast cancer on the moral nature, it attracts to itself and affects every ill humor of the soul.

To call into exercise this instinct for gain, the world now presents solicitations in number and force such as it never offered before. It presents them at every turn in life, and to all classes and conditions of men. The whole heart of society, especially in our own land, is inflamed with the passion for gain; it is the one literal maelstrom into which all forces, social and political, are drawn with a resistless power, and from which religion itself does not wholly escape.

Were this a passion that, like anger, blazing out, in due time consumes itself, then its ravages in the individual and social heart might be left to the healing offices of time. But no, this is a passion that, once seated in the soul, draws and enlists in its willing and life-long service every energy of the personal being. It even invokes religion to its aid, setting religion at defiance, however, whenever it cannot subordinate it to its service. It is a passion that is never lulled into rest, feeding and thriving on whatever comes in its way; and, unlike every other passion, becoming strongest when every other is cooled by the frosts of age.

And as with the individual, so with society; the passion for wealth is always cumulative. With the individual, every addition to the means of gratifying it, adds to the eagerness of desire for another; and with society, the great successes of the few inflame to fever heat the passion of the many. With the individual, death alone brings the passion to an end; in society, its end is only in upheaval, in overthrow, in revolution and reconstruction. History teaches us many lessons, but none more emphatically than that evils which spring from a soil made rich by the decay of religion and of morality and patriotism, can be cured only by the short, sharp remedy of social convulsions, — convulsions that leave ruins upon which long after, it may be, a revived faith in God and His moral laws can build anew. Most articulately is this lesson read to us by the Jerusalem and Rome that went down at the beginning of our era, under the selfishness and greed which had taken the place of the faith and virtues that once gave them their power and their glory.

Moral evils never exist singly; they are always gregarious. Inordinate love of wealth brings with it its troop of abundant vices. Out of the self-indulgence which wealth admits of, and to which it too often is made to minister, spring up an array of evil passions and vices which, like an army of locusts, eat the germs of every virtue of the soul. The lust of the flesh and the lust of the eyes are fed till, eating out the very core of being, the whole moral fabric, collapsing, falls a shapeless and hopeless ruin.

Again, associated with the inordinate love of wealth, sometimes as an effect and sometimes as a cause, and sometimes as that passion itself under a false guise, is the love of display, the craving for attention and notoriety, so characteristic of shallow minds and so alarmingly prevalent in our day and land. It is what the apostle John calls the pride of life, or more properly speaking, the vain-glory of life. It is the vain show in which empty souls so much delight to walk; it is rejoicing in the applause of others rather than in the quiet consciousness of self-approval; it is a craving for the credit of all we are and all we have done, and, alas, not infrequently, for the credit of being what we really are not. It is one of the vices of all times, but is pre-eminently one of the vices of our American society. The spirit of democracy specially fosters it. The political atmosphere of a republic in which every man is made to believe that he is the equal of every other, offers the most favorable conditions for its growth. A perpetual bribe is offered to the meanest and most unworthy to push themselves forward as claimants for all the honors due the noblest.

Christianity, under one aspect of it, is the great leveller of mankind; it places all men, king and subject, rich and poor, learned and unlearned, on the same footing before the eye of the great Searcher of Hearts. Under another aspect of it, Christianity is the great distinguisher or discriminator between men. It sets personal character in the clearest light, and awards to each what he is fittest to receive. It puffs up none, while by its inward enlightenment it humbles all. To dwell in its light is the one infallible cure for all vain-glory, whether of the individual or of the nation. Self-ignorance is the parent of pride, of presumption, and of vain-glory. Self-knowledge, and with it self-judgment, and so an unaffected humility, are the gifts of the religion of Christ and of His religion alone.

The final danger to which we shall allude is, in a sense, the outcome of all others; it is a disposition to be content with the semblance of character even when there is no reality of personal worth. This is one of the perils of all generations; it never needed to be more guarded against than in our day. Against it every principle of the Gospel puts us on our guard. If there be one characteristic to which Christianity attaches pre-eminent importance, it is that every man at the centre of his being shall actually be precisely what he professes to be. Reality at the very bottom of the soul is the one foundation-stone without which it will never proceed to build. Genuineness of character is the one requisite without which Jesus Christ will recognize the discipleship of no one. And all men hate hypocrisy in others; all are indignant when imposed upon by shams of character in other people.

But contentment with reputation instead of character is one of the commonest, as well as the most fatal, of the faults of our modern life. Many causes have contributed to its creation. Unbelief and the divorce of religion from morality prepare the way for it, the craving for wealth and the vain-glory which the possession of wealth often inspires, gives strength to it when once in existence. The publicity now given to the sacred privacies of life and the new function of the personal interviewer, all prompt to keep up appearances, to make a fair show for the eyes of others, whatever may be the real state of the inner man and of his private life. To suppose that publicity of life will insure transparency of character, or that to have all eyes turned on one will compel sincerity of heart, is to suppose what neither good sense nor experience warrants. The fact is that the temptation to put on appearances, to build up an imposing pasteboard front, will be strong just in proportion to the need there is for appearing well in the eyes of men. No man more needs to watch and fight against the demon of pretence than he who courts reputation, or who seeks some boon dependent on the good-will of others.

Gentlemen of the Graduating Class: You have come to the close of your academic training, to the duties of manhood and citizenship, at a period of the world's history when every energy of your being is summoned into activity, and when you will need all the discretion and decision of which you are capable. You enter upon the active duties of life when nothing, whether of sentiment or of institution, is regarded as too sacred for scrutiny and criticism. No human opinion and no divine thought are now regarded as having any right to be listened to till they have vindicated themselves at the bar of reason. Truth and error now have a free field on which to unfurl their banners for a final conflict. To the one side or the other in this conflict you will find yourself irresistibly drawn. There can be no neutrals and there can be no idle spectators.

But you need not be discouraged by the prospect of what is before you. Every generation must have its own dangers; those are the least to be dreaded which are the most clearly foreseen.

Let me beg you, then, first of all, to understand the time in which you live. It is a time of transition; a time in which the forms of things but not their substances are changing; when new thoughts demand recognition from the old; when Science forces itself on the attention of Philosophy, and when both Science and Philosophy, joining hands, insist that Religion shall listen to what they have to say. He alone is safe at such a time, who, with reverent spirit, seeks only to know the truth, standing ever ready with undivided heart to submit himself to its control.

Beware of a settled spirit of doubt, partly because of the disquiet, partly because of the moral enervation it is sure to breed; but chiefly because of the moral blindness it never fails to inflict. The habitual doubter is like the owl that hoots and hunts its prey only in the dark, and is always blindest when the light is brightest. From the very necessity of your nature you will need some kind of faith; consciously or unconsciously you will lean on some kind of support. But is there any higher than the Infinite God in whom you can believe, or, is there any foundation for your hopes surer than that which Jesus Christ has laid?

Let me remind you that the moral laws which are wrought into every fibre of your being will demand their fulfilment. They are laws which bind you at the one end to the eternal God, and at the other to your fellowmen. And they are laws the fulfilment of which, in one light, are morality and in another religion,—a morality which, without religion, is unreal, and a religion which, without morality, is futile.

You now go forth in pursuit of the prizes of life. Seek those only which are worthy of pursuit, which, when attained, will not disappoint you. If wealth comes to you by legitimate means, be thankful for it, and use it not for the gratification of the lust of the flesh, the lust of the eyes, and the pride of life, but for the good of mankind. Remember,—

>"'That from the body of one guilty deed
>A thousand ghostly fears and haunting thoughts proceed;"

that,—

>" Whose mind is but the mind of his own eyes,
>He is a slave, the meanest we can meet."

If reputation comes in recognition of good deeds, and just character, be neither ashamed of it nor unduly elated by it, and never forget that he who *seeks* it may find it to-day and lose it to-morrow; that the people who may be ready to crown you a king while they think you can help them to their selfish ends, will be the first to cry " crucify him " if you but cross them in their wishes.

But there is one end in life which may be pursued with a patience and a persistency that never need tire, with a self-sacrifice that need know no limit, and with a confidence that no discouragement need weaken; and that end is a character founded on truth and built up in accordance with the counsels of the eternal God. This will be a possession as inalienable as personal identity. Good men and angels and God will approve it. But be assured there is but one principle that can crystallize all thoughts and all feelings and all purposes and all affections into the solidity and symmetry and beauty of a character which will abide, and that principle is an honesty of soul which shrinks from no light, and is never so much at rest as when under the eye of Him who " looketh not on the outward appearance, but on the heart."

FAITH AND SENSE.

Fight the good fight of faith.
1 Timothy vi. 12.

THESE words are not to be taken in any narrow sense; they are not to be interpreted as an injunction to make faith the sole principle of action in life, nor to throw all our thoughts into another and future and invisible world, to the exclusion of this world; they give no hint of antagonism between what has been called " this worldism " and " other worldism; " they enjoin us to give to faith, in objects which it alone can comprehend, an ascendancy over the objects of sense; they present a conception of life as a continual conflict between sense and faith. The injunction is that we take care to fight earnestly against the objects of sense, in behalf of the objects of faith. There are many objects of faith that have no manner of influence over our lives. It makes little difference with us, or with our conduct or character, whether we believe in the solidity or fluidity of the earth's centre. But there are objects of faith which do concern us in our moral and spiritual life, and the teaching of the text is, that we struggle to make those objects of faith real, and to accomplish in us what they are intended to accomplish. That product of life which we call character will be thus formed and influenced.

Because, you know, every man becomes like what he believes, and the invisible power of a man's faith brings into his heart all the good, and takes out from it all the evil of that in which he trusts. If he trusts in objects below him, all the good in him goes out to those objects, and the evil in those objects is transferred to him; so that, if you know distinctly what a man believes, you may know his character. Every man, by necessity, becomes eventually what the faith of his nature is. And the fight is not for principles alone, but for ends of life.

First, then, we may ask, are these objects of faith real? Does faith lay hold of reality, or is it mere credulity? What are the invisible objects which we are urged to believe in? They are traits of character, purity of heart, personal integrity, wholeness and wholesomeness of soul, the thoughts and motives which make up the true man. We cannot perceive these attributes by any of our natural senses. Do you believe in them? If you do, do you know or do you not, when you attain unto them? Does any man doubt if he has purity of heart? Suppose it be integrity of soul; you believe in it. Why? Not because your senses grasp it, but because of intuitive evidences, — the evidences of faith. We are frequently told that sensible men believe only what their senses grasp. But I tell you that traits of character are all matters of faith, and that in our judgment of them we daily act on faith.

But, again, God is believed in by faith. We are urged to have faith in God. There are two phases of this belief: first, the belief merely that God exists, and secondly, that He exists with personal attributes. Lack of the first belief rarely occurs. The real atheist is a monster, and not often found. All men, practically, believe in the existence of some Supreme Being. It is the existence of a personal God and of His personal relations to us that is sometimes denied. But to the soul experiencing that God is a protecting Father, an Answerer of prayer, is there any doubt? If peace of mind is asked for and received, is it a reality? Is there any doubt as to that peace which passeth understanding? We are also asked to "believe on the Lord Jesus Christ,"— not to believe merely that Christ existed, for history proves that, — but to believe and trust in His power to save. When a soul, burdened with a sense of guilt, overcome by the power of evil, and sighing for deliverance, finding all blank in the world without, and all confused within himself, cries out, "O God, give me strength to conquer," and the sense of spiritual comfort and relief comes, is there any doubt about it? Are these objects certain or uncertain, real or unreal? Are we credulous or have we a rational trust? So I might proceed with other objects of faith. These, we claim, are real, and we believe in them because they are real.

But, secondly, "What certainty is there that we all may triumph in the conflict of faith and sense?" This is a question that every young man will ask. I answer, first, that faith itself is witness to the triumph assured. If an object of sense gratifies me, it acquires power over me. The force of habit is an illustration. So, if my eye be opened to discern the objects of faith, then those objects gratify my spiritual nature, my spiritual discernment, as distinguished from my natural vision. I am aware that I talk to some as vainly as if I were to speak to a South African Kaffir of the beauties of art. The natural eye cannot discern spiritual things. Spiritual things are spiritually discerned, and only so discerned. Let the spiritual capacity of the man be awakened and be put at work, and the soul comprehends the objects of faith. There is a parallel in the teaching of a child; the eye of the understanding is opened. A belief in learning obtains mastery over the child's senses, and he progresses in knowledge. And so, if you give the soul a taste of spiritual things, it will grow in spiritual knowledge, and the objects of faith, once apprehended, will give faith the mastery over sense.

Compare, if you will, the progress of faith with the progress of the senses. The eye, the ear, the hand, etc., all wear out. The objects into contact with which the senses bring us, soon lose their power, even the most entrancing of them. But the principle of faith grows stronger with each day's experience; the slender thread becomes a cable, and holds, in spite of all the world-storms which beat on the soul. Many have known what faith is, and what earthly experience is; they can testify how the world fades away, and how faith leads on to victory. We strive for the objects of sense, alas! how often in vain! The farmer toils from morn till sunset, but too much moisture or too much drought may ruin his harvest. The merchant lays his plans and is sure of rich returns, but his hopes vanish amid financial disaster. The scholar applies himself with unceasing perseverance, and shattered nerves, a disordered brain, a ruined digestion may be the result. Nothing earthly is absolutely certain; nothing that the senses can grasp is sure to endure. But what faith deposits in the soul abides. Even from the man bowed down by evil habits, not one earnest sigh goes up to Heaven but that it reacts upon his soul to nerve him and make him stronger. What you call character is made up of these appeals to God, these endeavors to do right, this trust in the objects of faith. Not the least cry for Divine help ever fails of its reflex influence and its direct answer. You say you strive vainly to follow Christ, but not one man or woman fails ultimately in realizing the effect of belief in objects of faith. The victory is certain.

But that victory is not easy; the struggle for it is justly called a fight. It is a desperate struggle, — many fail to understand how desperate, — this conflict between the senses and faith. It requires not only patience and self-denial, but often calls for sacrifice that wrings men's souls. Like the brave men who, in the siege at Cremona in the fourteenth century, when their treacherous enemy stole their children and marched towards them with those children in front of the line, yet struck down the foe even at the sacrifice of the children, for the sake of country, the devotee of faith must stop at no sacrifice in worldly concerns, holding in reserve not even the dearest interests of life. No triumph is certain without the willingness thus to sacrifice. Let there be no misunderstanding. No annihilation, no extermination of the senses is demanded, no violation of the laws of nature. Christ nowhere interferes with natural conditions. God and nature are one. Christ and nature are in harmony. The senses are the rounds in the ladder to faith. The man who would make of the ladder seats in which to loiter for earthly pleasure, is the man who sells his birthright for the objects of sense, who ruins his soul in the vanities of the world. True Christianity gives faith the ascendancy over the senses.

In conclusion, it may be asked, what is the value of the victory spoken of? What shall I gain, if I make the principle of faith superior to the senses? I reply, first, that there is a sufficient reward, if you prefer that term, even at the very close of life. There are times in the lives of all men when the essence of life is concentrated into a single moment. A long lifetime of storm ceases, and the clouds lift for a season, and a brief gleam of sunshine from the Sun of Righteousness fills the soul. You will recall the scene in the old Roman prison, where lay a man decrepit, blinded, and bearing the marks of heavy suffering, the howl of fierce wild beasts, starved that they might be the fiercer, falling upon his ear,—a man who had escaped the perils of sea, and robbery and scourging, the man who spoke the words of the text; you will recall his dictation of the closing words of his life: "The time of my departure is at hand. I have fought a good fight, I have kept the faith." Was not Paul's triumph in that hour sufficient compensation for all that he had suffered? I say here and now that, compared with such a moment of victory at the close of life, all trials are as nothing. Another grander scene will come to mind, the loftiest scene that ever angels or men beheld,—that under the olive-tree in the garden by the walls of Jerusalem, when arose that sublimest prayer that ever went up to Heaven: "Father, the hour is come.

... I have finished the work which Thou gavest me to do." It is true that we may never reach these sublime heights, but we may approach them.

What success do the objects of sense secure? Not one of your worldly acquisitions can you take to the life beyond. But when the closing hour comes, character is as inseparable from the soul as its own identity; it is as abiding as the throne of God. The humblest human being who sends up the cry, "O God, be merciful," will take into his soul that which is his own forever, and of which nothing can rob him. I have said, then, that the objects of faith are real and abiding. I submit if they are not more to be desired than all else in comparison.

Gentlemen of the Graduating Class: No question can be more momentous for you at this hour, as you are about to step out into the life of the world, than that suggested in the theme of the afternoon: Whether you will render allegiance to the objects of sense, or lay hold of that life which discerns the objects of faith. You cannot be indifferent to this question. If you waive it, you will yield unconsciously to the senses; if you shut your eyes and ears to faith, you will find the whole atmosphere of modern life full of baits for the senses, and before you are aware of it you will be enslaved. It is possible for any one of you to make a wreck of life, to go down in mid-ocean an irrecoverable loss; but it is possible also for you to open the eye of the soul and the ear of the heart to the objects of faith. He who follows the latter course, walks in the clear light of day. God has made you freemen, not slaves, and has stamped you with something of

His own character. The question is, which course will you choose in life? In the months past we have together given our attention to study of the unchanging laws of being which hold every one of us. We can change them no more than we can change our identity. Will you obey those laws? You alone must answer. Pardon me, if, as your teacher, I charge you, in the presence of these witnesses, in the presence of the All-seeing God, who knows your every thought,— as your friend and teacher, I charge you, rise above your senses; lay hold of the objects of faith. Live worthily and patiently. The objects of faith are real. Victory is certain if you comply with the conditions. Be sure that everything of this world is worth naught at the close of life. The end of life will be disappointment unutterable, if you have not faith. Take hold of the things that are eternal, break through the control of the senses. So live that, when life is done, you may feel that your work is accomplished. God alone knows which one of you will go first. Not long hence some of you must leave the body. God help you so to live that when the end comes you may be able to say, "I have fought a good fight, I have kept the faith," and may there thenceforth be laid up for you a crown of righteousness above.

THE LIFE WORTH LIVING.

I have fought a good fight.
2 TIMOTHY iv., part of 7th verse.

THESE were the words of a man who was about to end his days at the hands of the public executioner. He had lived a life of incessant toil, of severest hardships, of bitterest persecution; and yet it was with no repining that he looked back upon that life. Indeed, there is in his words an unmistakable tone of exultation. It was a glad and grateful retrospect that met his eye as he glanced backward; he was content with the results of a life so ending.

When men fight, if they are intelligent persons, they fight for a definite object. The ignorant herd of soldiers may fight merely for their stipend, merely to please their leaders. But the projectors of all wars have great and definite objects to fight for. The apostle had fought distinctly for a purpose; that purpose had been achieved. What it was, is well known to you all. From the animating Source of that life there sprang a "stream of tendency" that, coming down the centuries, is to-day moving onward with increasing volume, with resistless energy, — spreading out, with its fruitful tide, over this whole earth.

Exactly to imitate that life is impossible for any one now. But to live worthy of one's endowments, one's opportunities, is possible for all men. A fitting life is as possible to-day as ever. What is, then, a fitting life for men? What is an object for which it is worth our while to arm ourselves, standing on our guard and fighting to the death? Let the answering of that question be the object of our brief reflection at this time. What is a fitting life to be lived?

Doubtless, first of all, it may be said, for every man to make the utmost possible — admissible by his endowments — of himself; to develop himself into the largest possible manhood; so to expand every power in harmony with every other as that the highest ideal man shall be attained. But every human being is compounded of a variety of forces, — forces which must be kept in careful adjustment, or disorder is inevitable; forces that fall into discord, if but for a moment there is lost the control of them which reason is designed to exercise. Thus, it is the simplest possible thought that man has a body, that he has an intellect, and that he has affections. This bodily organism is, on every side, at every turn in life, met with solicitations to call it into exercise. The senses are appealed to every moment of our being. Yielding to the senses, — senses that were intended to be bitted and bridled, and guided and controlled, the man is enslaved; the angel that is in him yields to the beast, — for we are allied both to the beast and to the angel; we are two-fold, and he who for a moment yields to the control of the senses sinks to sensuality. Or, he may rise above the sensuous; he may employ his intellect upon the numberless objects which meet his eye whatever way he turn. All the powers which constitute him rational may be brought into play. He cannot turn his eyes to the heavens but they speak to him; he cannot look at the earth beneath him but it calls into exercise his thought. The voices that are in him and around him, everywhere, summon him to manly exercise. The intellectual may occupy him, or, social as we are, the affections may absorb and control all. In either case, man is one-sided; he is not fully developed. Each must have its share. We may attempt to bring the intellect into the mastery by doing violence to the senses, — to the instincts and appetites with which each human being is endowed. The instincts and appetites will avenge themselves for the wrong. You may deny their gratification, and they will turn again and rend you. Or you may call upon the intellect, and, urging it on its service, you may starve the appetites and the affections, and you will become "an intellectual machine." The earth has known many such; they are but half-men. And then there are your sentimentalists, whose unhealthy affections are fed and fostered till they sink below the human standard; they are neither men nor women.

The question then at once propounds itself: "What constitutes the largest expansion of this human personality?" To let each particular force with which God has endowed us perform its specific office, healthfully, consistently, that the whole personal being may be rounded out into that ideal completeness which constitutes the real "image of God."

But here we are at once told that "the highest end in life is something else than to make the most of *self*." It is to obtain the largest measure of enjoyment; it is, to use a colloquial phrase, "to get the most possible out of life." Under different terms this is put before men. At one time it is dignified by the term "happiness;" at another it is called "pleasure." What is happiness? Make it, if you will, the distinct object of your pursuit, and so certain as you do, you never will attain it. The men who make the pursuit of happiness the controlling object of life are the men who

"Never *are*, but always *to be* blest,"

and they who stop and inquire, "Am I not now happy?" find that the very instant they look within, to ascertain whether happiness exists, like bottled fragrance, it has vanished. The instant you attempt to analyze and determine if you are now happy, your happiness is gone. No man ever found it by asking himself, "Have I not now found it?" It is always unconscious; it is always the result, not of searching, but the result of attainment of that which is searched for. I do not forget what the profound German thinker said when he declared that if the Almighty were to meet him, holding truth in one hand, and "search for truth" in the other, and propose to him his choice, that he would select "search for truth," rather then truth itself. Possibly philosophic truth is never attainable, and the highest happiness of man is to be in pursuit of it. Possibly we are so constituted that we are satisfied and delighted only when we are moving on with unimpeded energy. But the conditions of true happiness are his only whose whole being is so organized and co-ordinated in its forces, that each particular part is in harmonious action with every other part. The happiest being that treads this earth of God is that being whose whole personal nature is so ordered that unconsciously every part performs its function without observation or without reflection; and he who is the possessor of such a personal life is the man who is most truly blest of God, — not having *sought* his happiness, but unexpectedly *found* it.

But we shall be here reminded that it is selfishness still, even when self-expansion and self-development are the objects of pursuit; that we are thinking only of *ourselves*. We shall be reminded, in the modern jargon of scientific speech, that there is a constant conflict between " egoism " and " altruism," between " self-ism " and " other-ism. " Let us remember that no human being ever attains to the largest expansion of his nature except by continuously remembering his connection with the rest of the human race. All that now is, is the result of the past. The human race is a continuity; it is a personality; it is *one*. What we have " entered into " is the result of untold struggles, conflicts without number, martyrdoms, sacrifices, slaughters, upbuilded and overthrown cities. Think, if you can, of the gigantic, of the melancholy, but of the grand march of humanity through this world's history, from the impenetrable darkness of the past into the full noon-day of this hour; for what we call our civilization, what we call our blessedness of opportunity, is simply the result of all the past. We have " entered into " it. They who preceded us, in apostolic language, could not be " perfect " without us. So of the future; all that is to come is, in the germ, in us. The future is *here;* it is in our trust. As we cannot sever ourselves from the past, so by no possibility of thought can any man sever himself from the years to come. We look back upon our progenitors, and we either bless or curse. Our posterity will rise up and bless or curse us according to our heed or unmindfulness of those who are to come after us. So that there can be no true self-expansion, no enlargement of being, and therefore, no real happiness for the man who forgets his relation to this human race of which he is a part.

And then, furthermore, we must also bear in mind our relation to the generation that now is. We must fight, as of God, against the adverse influences with which we are surrounded; they are ever with us. You may call it the "spirit of this world;" name it by whatever name you will, it exists; and no human being can make the most of himself, except as he stands on guard against the temptations which meet him in society, — temptations to obtain wealth, to achieve position, to secure power, by the sacrifice of what is purest and best in his nature. Not alone this, but human society cannot influence a man safely. Why, our human race is to-day what it always has been, — moved now by freak, now by passion; its fashions are freaks; its customs are unnatural growths. We are not speaking of the courtesies, the amenities of society, which soften and refine men, but of its allurements and corruptions, which never help any man into the rounding out of himself into the fulness of manhood. You remember the vehement protest of that clear-headed, strong English thinker, John Stuart Mill, when he wrote that book on "Liberty," — a vehement protest against the influence of society, against the domination of the common customs of men: "The multitudes of men and women that are warped through fear, — fear of ridicule, fear of sly remark, fear of unfriendly criticism! The man that would have self-respect, that would attain to true manhood, must know the dignity of personal being, must dare to stand up and do right, whatever the multitude may say or do." Because the multitude, in ninety cases out of a hundred, are wrong. The majority, I may say, are almost always in the wrong. The right is with the clear-headed minority.

But it is not alone in fighting against the adverse influences of society. We must fight against the temptations to neglect society, to despise it, to stand aloof from it. That is especially one of the dangers of the educated man, who lives in his closet, who thinks with the past, who raises himself above what he sometimes calls " the vulgar herd." How shall he protect himself? You remember that the greatest of all the Greek philosophers, in his treatise on Ethics, sets forth with glowing language " the great-souled man," — the soul lifting itself up into the conception of the noble, the sublime, the grand, the heroic. The Latins have translated it naturally into *magnanimitas*. Out of it has come our word " magnanimity." How vast the difference between the great-souledness — the original of that term with old Aristotle — and the meaning of that word to-day. Your " great-souled " man, gathering up his clean skirts around him, lest they shall be tainted by contact with the rude and vulgar world, moves through society with magnificent tread, with lofty thought, with high aims, but forgets his fellowmen, to help whom he and each individual being has been summoned into existence. To-day, as in the olden time, magnanimity is "great-souledness," but great-souledness condescending to the lowest estate, pitying the pitiable, stretching out the helping hand. How have we learned it from that great Example for men and angels to gaze at, when He stooped to open blind eyes, to unstop deaf ears, to raise the dead, to heal the sick, walking forth in the earth, great-souled, but condescending and gentle and self-forgetful. This is the indispensable condition of attaining to the largest development of our nature. There are parts of our nature that are called into being, there are sensibilities, there are the subtile graces, which nothing but contact with wretchedness can call out, nothing but pity can summon into exercise. The man, therefore, that everywhere goes forth and tries to alleviate human distress, is the man that is taking the most direct steps toward making the utmost possible of himself. Do you think that John Hampden, when he staked his estate, his name, all that his ancestry had handed down, in his determined opposition to the encroachments of the king, lowered himself? Do you think that Clarkson and Wilberforce, when they stood serenely before the storm of contempt which they met in the British Parliament, declaring that slavery was a thing accursed of God and should cease to be, — do you think that they in those acts descended? Did they do otherwise than build themselves up into the largest manhood? So of *the human* in man everywhere.

But here again we shall be told that what you call "benevolence," this doing good to others, is, after all, but a disguised form of selfishness. That is the modern statement. That is what Christian people are now told, — that benevolence, doing good to others, is only a disguised form of self indulgence. The mother who tears the cloak from her shivering shoulders, that she may protect her freezing child, acts selfishly. She gratifies an inward instinct. The gratification of the maternal instinct, it is said, is a subtle form of selfishness. The young hero who springs from the deck of the ocean steamer, in the middle of the Atlantic, to rescue a drowning child, is acting selfishly. But what about the one hundred and one that stand clinging to the bulwarks of the vessel, looking over, content with their empty sighs of pity? Let a whole vessel-load of passengers be scattered upon the waves of the sea, and another vessel-load of passengers be sailing by, will they all jump overboard to rescue the drowning? Is that a disguised form of selfishness? Does not all the world recognize the fact that the forgetting of self is something sublime; that it is not a disguised form of self-indulgence; that it is self-sacrifice; that it exalts; that it brings into play all the subtile, higher forces of man, and so develops them as to round them out into the completest ideal of manhood?

But I may here be asked, "What is to control us, in this battle of life, in trying to make the utmost possible of ourselves? What shall nerve us with energy in the fight? What, in common language, shall be the one grand motive of all our action? What is to lie behind us and nerve us for the conflict?" One says: It is what human society has determined to be fittest for man, for his highest development. But what is " human society " ? Simply a collection of individuals. Their opinion is no more than my own private opinion. Suppose some one comes to me and says: "Here, it has been voted by all men that self-sacrifice is nobler than self-indulgence;" if I, in my thought, conclude that self-indulgence is nobler than self-sacrifice, I can pit my opinion against theirs. Men are constantly doing it. But another says: "It is found in the conflict between different kinds of happiness." On the one hand, is the happiness of self-indulgence. Why, men sink back into that lowest form of human life where they say: "I will simply surrender to my appetites, — the brutal, the enslaved, the bestial form of humanity, — where I am perpetually seeking to gratify these appetites of mine, vacating my manhood, forfeiting my birthright, blotting out the image of Himself that God gave to me." On the other hand, is the happiness of self-sacrifice, the blessedness of the man who feels that he has sacrificed himself that he may bless another; like the hungry man who, coming to his dinner, sees the starving tramp, and hands it to him, and afterwards says, "I have saved a victim from death." It may be said that that is a vague satisfaction; pit one against the other, and ninety-nine out of every hundred of our human race will say, "Give me the present gratification." You cannot balance pleasures. No one has ever yet succeeded in balancing them, and when our modern philosophers tell us about altruism and egoism, that they are balanced one against the other, and that so the human race is kept in a state of equilibrium, the truth is that men will sacrifice this race of ours, if left alone simply to their choice between self-indulgence and self-sacrifice.

Some one will come forward — there are such — and say to you, "Friend, what you seek is not in your idea of manhood, in your development. It is not in benevolence; it is simply a matter of strong, silent submission to law, to the mechanical laws that rule in this world." They tell us that the man who surrenders himself to the teachings of science is intellectually honest; that he never asks, "What ought I to find?" "Find out what is; find out what is," they tell us. This is the gospel of the day. "Find out, by your careful observation, what now is, and, having ascertained the law, gird yourselves up, with true manhood, to bow before it, asking no questions, parleying with no feelings, but simply asking of the law what it demands. Law to them is like the sphinx's face, — moveless, — no heart behind it, looking out grimly over the waste sands of life; and the man who acts simply from law vacates his affections, surrenders his will, makes himself but one of the cogwheels of this universe, becomes purely a part of the mechanism. And there are men, types of this kind of manhood, stepping forth now as grand examples. What are they? They certainly are not sensuous. They have sacrificed all self-indulgence; their God is science; they bend all their energy to find out what is; they are men that have lifted themselves up above all that you could call low or degrading. But what are they?

> "Faultily faultless; icily regular; splendidly null."

Like statues, as unmoving and unmoved as the marble or the bronze statue of your market-place; as unmoved and unmoving amid the sacrifices and sufferings of our race as the statues that grace the solitary places of the parks. They have not that loving, that loyal recognition of the wants and the needs of their fellowmen, which Christianity enjoins, which tells you: " Make the most you can of yourselves, but make it in the sacrifice of yourselves for the good of others. Forgetting self, you will find self. Benefiting others, you will attain to the truest dignity of your nature."

It is not, therefore, in the conflict of laws that a man is to find the grand motive-power which shall nerve him for life's battle. What, then, is it? I know but one thing. Upon all this conflict of motives, this turmoil of passion, there comes the voice of One who declares, " All this is My creation. I am God, and beside Me there is none other." The conscience, — *that* speaks with authority. There is no authority in law, to man, unless that law express a personal will; no authority in your Sphinx's riddle; no authority in these phenomena of nature, — unless they express a personal will lying behind them. And when that personal will, representing to us supreme, loving authority, commands that we sacrifice ourselves for the good of man, and for the honor of God, then, in obeying, do we recognize a power that transforms us, lifts us up, puts a new spirit into our souls, enables us to look upon life as God intended it to be viewed, — a life of conflict, a life of struggle, a life ending in triumph. We recognize one God, who ever lives and loves; one God, one law, one element, one far-off divine event, to which the whole creation moves. To that God, to that creation, to that law, let us all be now and ever loyal — submitting, worshipping, toiling, loving, living on, assured of a triumphant ending.

Gentlemen of the Graduating Class: I need not continue these words farther than to ask you to remember and apply to yourselves the principles we have now discussed. The substructions of your personal characters are already laid; the superstructure to be built upon them must be strictly in accordance with your own will and working. What shall it be? You can easily gather up the loose materials that the world piles around you, and build a kind of character. Or, you can build from materials gathered only by your own patient quarrying; you can build with materials that will survive those fiery tests to which everything human must at times be subjected. Things that live are only of to-day; to-morrow is yet to be born. The past is ever dead and dying. Learn, first of all, then, to " make stepping stones of your dead selves to higher things." Let nothing past suffice; ever onward, and ever upward! In life you will meet many and disguised temptations. They will come to you gilded, will thrust themselves upon you at every turn in life. It will be easy for you to be betrayed; nothing but watchfulness will keep you, — nothing but an undying determination to stand ever on your guard, ready for a fierce conflict for the right. God give you strength to fight always for truth; to fight always for the right, for self-respect, for God, for universal righteousness. And on the earnestness with which you fight, though men misunderstand and forget, will depend the end. You will either be vanquished, or you will be victors. You must take your choice. You can be victors, every man of you, no matter what your surroundings, what your temptations, what your perils. It is now within your reach to make of yourselves true men; you have it in your power to surrender all. Couch, like Issachar, under the burdens of life, content with the things that are pleasant, and the world will trample on you with its rude hoofs, and shovel you into your graves, forgotten. But, remembering the truths with which you have here been growingly familiar, remembering the God who hath said to you, " Be faithful," the Christ who has taught you how to live, every one of you may achieve a life at the end of which you can lie down in peace, saying, " I have finished my course, and God be thanked that I have lived." Young gentlemen, I now and here charge you, as American citizens, as men who are to receive from your predecessors great trusts, as men who are enjoined of God to hand those trusts over to your successors, I now charge you never to bribe or be bribed to the wrong, never to surrender your manhood, nor your self-respect, to any temptation. And so certain as you observe this injunction, not an earnest purpose of yours for the right shall fail, not a deed faithfully done but shall leave its deposit in your soul, building up in the end a character that will please God, and will be to yourselves an eternal source of satisfaction. May your days be many; but whether they be many or few, be true, be faithful, and in the end, He who rules over all will crown you with that crown of righteousness with which the Apostle, whose words you have heard spoken to-day, was assured that his life should be crowned at the last.

TRUE WORSHIP.

*Thou shalt worship the Lord thy God, and **H**im only shalt thou serve.*

LUKE iv. 8.

EVERY man has some one object of supreme regard, — an object around which the thoughts of his life revolve. Other subordinate ideas accompany it as contributive, but not as central ideas. Great revolutions occur sometimes in individual experiences, and there is a change in the supreme object; tributary objects sometimes become supreme over all. A devotion to inferior ends is sometimes called worship. A man may worship art, nature, ideas, or beauty, but our text calls attention to the word worship, not in an allowable or metaphorical sense, but in the highest sense, as devotion to God.

There are many elements in what we call worship. The lowest is admiration; and from admiration it may ascend to the highest adoration, the true worshp of God. True worship is an awakening to highest praise and devout adoration. We are called on in our text for true worship. True worship is a surrender of our entire being to God; it is not simply to praise Him, but to serve Him with body and spirit. True worship is a spontaneous expression of intelligence. The higher the intelligence, the more profound is the worship. It is ignorance that is bold. Ignorance is bold, irreverent, and reckless, because it does not know what worship to God is. The educated man who has true knowledge, sees and hears, and comprehending, bows in reverent worship. Intelligence and worship come from those whose knowledge and experience is widest.

I choose the words of the text because they were quoted by Christ, and have been reiterated down the ages to the present time. In reading the Psalms, you will notice that the writers declare that all nature recognizes and praises God. We bow before these gifts of life which surround us, and go into raptures over the beauties of the sky, the earth, and the sea; but we do not bow before them for themselves. Everything in nature embodies an idea; men are recognizing these ideas. These things are not simply to make life pleasant; they speak to us, and we gather from them our sciences. Sum these sciences into the one comprehensive thought that all nature reveals and praises God, and we instinctively cry out with the Psalmist, "Worship the Lord thy God." This world is ruled by silent, irresistible, multifarious, multitudinous forces, all working out a unity of ends. They bring out order from chaos, all working by inflexible laws. In this beautiful June weather the very skies speak out to us, exhorting us to bow down before God.

Every nation reflects in character the Deity it worships, and every nation has its Deity. You study the history of a people; you know the Deity they worship. You analyze it, and you know their character. Analyze their character, and you know their Deity. The Puritan God made deep and hard lines on the character of the English people which no revolution has erased or can efface. So every nation must have a character in accordance with the character of its Deity. The inner thought of man will respond to the thought that "righteous and just are thy judgments, O God." Looking over the experiences of the past and present, and looking into the future, we know that God rules righteously. As His judgments go forth at the last, our hearts will respond that they are just and true.

There are two distinct ways of worshipping God. One is by the observance of religious rites in public worship. I know of no symptom of our time that should awaken profounder alarm than that so large a proportion of the living people fail to engage in public worship, and that there is such a multitude of educated men who never appear or participate in assemblies singing praises and offering worship to God. Worship of God is not a petition. A profane oath is a petition, but is not worship. All over our land are educated men who all their lives have been gathering God's gifts, and who never deign to meet God's people. Is there not something for them in the service which raises a man above his sordid desires, influences him to clothe himself in clean linen, and to divest himself of all that degrades and soils, and to seek enlightenment from communion with Him who filled the world with beauty and joy? What man has not been, by the worship of God, lifted and strengthened in heart to bear his burdens and fight the battles of faith, righteousness, and truth. Do the men who bargain their consciences for high political position bow down and worship God? When such people talk the cant of "worshipping nature," they know in their hearts they are not honest Christians, and are not such men as will go to God and say, "Thou hast called us; let us be Thy servants." Let us rather speak the word in the regular assembly, singing hymns of praise and adoration, and striking hands for righteousness and truth. This church service is something which fits men for the outer and public life; observing it, they catch glimpses of their hidden motives, of their nearness to God, of inevitable rewards and retributions which fill them with awe, and the fear to commit unrighteous deeds. He who presents his brief at the bar, he who ministers to the sick, he who is God's minister, he who bargains, he who embarks in great enterprises and commerce, are led to say, not with cant and hypocrisy, "God guide me and help me to fulfil the obligations imposed on me in life." This is true service, a reverent regard for God and conscience continued through all the ramifications of life, in the domestic circle, in business, alone with God, and among men in His public worship.

[Dr. Robinson then addressed the graduating class substantially as follows:—]

The stage of life which you enter upon stands enveloped in profound and inscrutable mystery. The future, which has no ending, is before you; if you should take the wings of thought and try to fly to the uttermost limits of space, your mind would tire, and seek a resting-place. But in boundless space and through all time God is, always has been, and always will be. His will is written in laws on your minds and hearts, and speaks to you and holds you.

As you enter upon a new stage of life, numberless prizes are set before you, never so great, so tempting, or so easily reached as to-day. You enter at a time when all the accumulated opportunities and treasures of the past are poured forth in innumerable and enticing forms. Satan invites you to fall down and worship him, and promises that all the kingdoms of the world shall be yours. You will be tempted, and I bid you remember what Jesus replied: "Get thee hence, Satan, for it is written thou shalt worship the Lord thy God, and Him only shalt thou serve." Whatever comes to you in your after life, there will always be a compensation, for nothing stands absolutely by itself. When you secure the prizes that men sacrifice themselves for, you will be oppressed with an unspeakable sense of their emptiness. There is one Being who can fill this void, — He who created the boundless universe and its infinite resources, to whom I bid you bow the knee, not in servile service, but as a son of God. As a true son of God, He offers you the fellowship of His Son, who will be to you as an Elder Brother in fighting the fight of faith. When forty or fifty years have passed, and you come to the solemn festivals of this college, only those who have been faithful to God in truth and righteousness, will be found to have truly prospered. Whatever may be your experiences in life, even if you fail, as men count it, be true to God and there can be no real failure. May the Infinite Being watch over you and help you to make His life yours.

NATURE AND REVELATION.

And I saw another angel fly in the midst of heaven, having the everlasting Gospel to preach unto them that dwell on the earth, and to every nation, and kindred, and tongue, and people, saying with a loud voice, "Fear God and give glory to Him; for the hour of His judgment is come; and worship Him that made heaven and earth, and the sea and the fountains of waters."

REVELATIONS xiv. 6, 7.

THE association of the works and the word of God in the Scripture is full of significance. It reminds us that what we distinguish as nature and revelation are not only from one and the same source, but exist for the same ends. He who created heaven and earth made them for a purpose. That same purpose is taken up and carried forward in the words spoken by the prophets and apostles, as well as by the works of nature. The methods by which these ends are sought differ. What we call nature works by what we in our ignorance call forces. The revelation of the Word of God proceeds by methods different from those of nature, but both reach their ends definitely and intelligently, and harmonize one with the other. What God purposes to accomplish by His works, He accomplishes also by His words, but by His works more slowly. There is not a sound but has a voice in it, a thought. That thought is plainly to be read by him who desires to know it. The prophets, by a single sentence, could predict the doom of a city or a nation. Nature moved slowly through centuries in accomplishing what the prophets in a sentence had uttered. But in the end nature and revelation are one.

This is eminently true of the Gospels. They are everlasting Gospels, not of a day nor of an hour, but for all time and all races. They interpret the word of God. They are not an unexpected appendix to complete a system, but a consummation of it. What nature does in a blind way, the Gospel of Christ does as the consummation of the purpose for which the universe exists.

Attempts have frequently been made, however, to set nature and revelation in antagonism; not only to divorce them, but to place one over against the other to supplant it. Let us glance at some of these attempts, confining ourselves to the last two and a half centuries. Two and a half centuries ago the attempt was made to supplant revelation by human reason, which was said to be enough for all man's necessities. Lord Herbert's attempt was the beginning of English deism, and ultimately of German rationalism. Whatever he intended, he simply put reason in place of revelation. But when this system had done its utmost, it found itself supplementing the very work that revelation was doing.

Reason had been ostracized by the believers in revelation as antagonistic to it, and overthrowing it. In the long period of English literature we find numerous intimations of the opposition of the two. We know what the results were. The reaction came. Reason is to show the reasonableness of the Scriptures, the reasonableness of Christianity; and to-day the two are in perfect harmony.

Subsequently there were other attempts of the same kind. It was declared that the voices of nature and of God were not in harmony, that one contradicted the other; and the different sciences in succession were appealed to. The first was astronomy. In the heavens men declared that they found a testimony to contradict the teachings of revelation. But in the course of time astronomy is found one of the most dutiful of the handmaidens of religion. Geology was no sooner born than it was brought to this service. Moses, it was affirmed, was mistaken. In course of time, however, though errors and discrepancies were found in detail, geology and revelation were seen to harmonize. So He who told of the creation of the world knew more of it than was seen on its surface. Passing to other sciences, there cannot be found one whose teachings are in opposition to revelation.

In physiology we were told that human consciousness is only a state of the brain, that feeling is only a thrill of the nerves. All that belongs to the human spirit was explained by the human organism. God was no longer discoverable in the human frame; there was nothing in the heavens; the heavens were empty; the earth was barren. It was sought to prove that all life is not created, but came out of the forces of nature. But the answer through the lengthening line of scientific inquiry is, that no explanation can be given of this universe except by that of a Creator who created the germs of all things. The most pronounced evolutionist admits that a primal cause is a necessary presupposition. The surprise is that germs containing within them all that we see in the full flavoring and fruitage of humanity come from an unknown and undiscoverable source. Science quits her search for spontaneous generation, and declares that somewhere, somehow, there is a first cause. Such have been the inquiries and such the results. We come back to the fact that whatever science teaches, revelation takes up and interprets.

What does science teach? That the laws of God are as unchangeable as God Himself; that in these laws there is a purpose — a will; and Christianity comes in as an interpreter and works in harmony with it. Does nature tell us in mumbling utterance that as we sow, so shall we reap? But it may take us long years to understand the teaching. God's word tells it to us in one sentence. If we are guilty of a violation of our physical constitution, we cannot avoid the penalties of nature. Christianity tells us exactly the same truth. Nature tells us in a faint voice how to escape in some measure the inevitable penalty. Christianity tells us that he who sins must die; but in Christianity is found the hope of salvation and recovery through belief in Jesus Christ.

Attempts have been made to discredit this truth by some of those who are alien to the Gospel of Christ. Unfortunately, there have arisen processes of thought and methods of interpretation by which the friends of Christianity take some foremost portion of its doctrine and dislocate and distort it. He who overstates a truth understates an error. Nothing is more dangerous than perverted truth. If you lift some facts of Christianity into undue prominence, you are guilty of error. The two most important elements of Christianity are faith and love. Faith is the most effective constructive principle of the Christian religion; for every man becomes unconsciously like what he implicitly believes in and seeks, by a law as inevitable as that of gravitation. Christianity adopts this principle, and every man is saved by faith. No truth is more self-evident, none more easy of vindication. Christianity proposes the faith in One who made His appearance on earth both as the Son of Man and the Son of God. He died for the race; but He died to save those who trust in Him. What is that trust? Not a process of the will by which you say, "I accept Him." It is not that alone; that is a mere work; something done. Alas! how frequently is that the only acceptance of Christ.

There are two causes to prevent any further and truer belief. The first is an earnest attempt to master the results of Christian teaching. Modern revelation seeks a quick return, as they say in trade. I make the statement, I believe in Him, and all is done. This is a perversion,—not faith, but a mistaken trust.

Another and corresponding element of Christianity is the principle of love. According to the teachings of God's word, love is the fulfilling of all law. Why? Because what occupies my thoughts and fills my attention moulds me. Love is not separable from faith. Love, they tell us, is the source of life, the great foundation of the universe. The question is put, will you not respond to Christ's love? Will you not love Him? And the answer immediately is, "Oh, yes; I love Him for all He is, for all He has done, for His gifts and benefits." How utterly unlike that stern declaration, "I love the laws of God!" We are told that Christ and Christianity were perverted in the past by too great emphasis on law and on justice. John Calvin, they tell us, was a great perverter of God's truth. He insisted that justice ruled the world; that Christ came to fulfil all righteousness. That, they tell us, produced Puritanism,—a stern and unlovely belief; and to-day, they say, is a day of unbounded rejoicing in love, which the greatest teacher of the nineteenth century has rescued and restored to its proper place.

But what did Jesus Christ tell us? "Till heaven and earth shall pass away, not one jot or tittle of the law shall be abated;" "If you love me keep my commandments." Read the Gospel of Christ, and see if it is the gospel of gushing emotion! See if it is not the doctrine of stern practical life. We are told it is a gospel of love and not of law and fear. What are the fruits of this teaching? Go back half a century; when a man was known to be a Christian man, his word was to be trusted. A defaulter was so rare in those days that his name was used to designate the crime. In twenty-five years what do we see? Church members and Sunday-school superintendents defaulters, and the name of a Christian no guarantee of honesty. These are the fruits. Whence come they? This suave gospel which forgets that the old world was built on law is the cause. We are told that Christianity is the gospel of forgiveness. To-day it is considered ill-bred to use the word hell. It is abolished: law has gone by. All this is the outgrowth of that system which partially denies and partly perverts our holy religion. For myself, I would a thousand times rather have the old Puritanism, with all its crabbedness and harshness, than this sentimentalism, this soft-flowing " quick return " religion, making it so easy to find the way into the kingdom of God, and as easy to find the way out of it.

Let us understand, however, that there is no truth greater or more precious than the truth which teaches that all men are saved by belief in Jesus Christ. God forbid that we say a word against love. But true love, Christian love, is seen in the fruits of the spirit; it is the upbuilder of character.

If what I say be true, then the declaration with which I opened is not untrue. The Gospel of Christ aims at the same thing as the creation of God; and they are not contradictory. Let us, therefore, understand that all divine processes are but one unchanging aim of God to teach men that God cares for us; that He works by unchanging laws, and in His work He changes not one of those laws. It is not more true that if physical laws cease, confusion and chaos will come, than that if we cease to regard the laws of God, truth, justice, and mercy, moral chaos will follow.

Gentlemen of the Graduating Class: You have now been associated together some four years in diligent study of the works of God. They have presented themselves to you in varied forms; in them all you have found laws. You have studied language, and found there laws immutable; you have studied the processes of thought, and discovered the laws of thought. You have turned your attention to the heavens and found laws. Mathematics have declared to you their immutable laws. You have studied the human organism, and there you find laws implacable. You have found in all and everywhere, proclaimed as by a voice eternal, that God is in all things. There is no escape from His laws, no evasion, no fleeing the penalty of their violation.

You are going into life, not one of you with any conception of the path you are to walk. Let your sole fear be a holy, reverent fear of God, who only requires you to take that step in the space which is open to you. Take it serenely, manfully, confidently. Remember one thing amid all your searchings, inquiries, aspirations,— everything in the world worth having is found in Jesus Christ. To Him commit your hearts, so that, as you fall out of the ranks, they will say of you: He lived faithful to His trust. May God guide you so to live.

SERVING ONE'S GENERATION.

For David, after he had served his own generation, by the will of God, fell on sleep, and was laid unto his fathers.
ACTS xiii. 36.

THIS was the epitaph of one of the most distinguished men of the earth, of one who had served his generation according to the will of God. David was one of the extremely few men in the world's history who have not only marked their character upon their times, but have moulded every generation following them. Reared as a shepherd, he yet organized, and virtually founded, the most distinguished kingdom our world has ever known. He also uttered words, the most ennobling, expressive of the loftiest aspirations that have ever moved the human soul.

Service to God and service to mankind may be separated in thought, but not in fact. To serve one's generation is to serve God, and to serve God is to serve one's generation. True religion and true philanthropy are never separated. It is proper, therefore, for us to set before ourselves the duty of serving our generation.

And, first, what does this service consist in? It does not consist in yielding to the whims of the generation; it does not consist in floating passively on the current of our time, nor in flattering our generation into the furtherance of our own plans, for this is serving ourselves, not our generation; neither does it consist in flattering our generation for the sake of applause. Popularity is easily attainable when one ministers to the wishes of people. He who simply, like a mirror, reflects his time, is the one whom people will applaud and follow. Contrast the careers of John Wilkes and Edmund Burke,— the former, the wily demagogue, with all London at his heels, Middlesex pushing him into Parliament, whence he had been rejected. Who knows him to-day? Burke, on the other hand, who, when he saw England drifting from her moorings lifted a loud voice of warning, has left a storehouse of thought from which men have been drawing treasures ever since. One was the most popular man of his time; the other was one of the most philosophical and far-sighted of men among the generations of England. Compare the contemporaries, Cowley and Milton, — the one popular, but a writer of puerile thoughts, a flatterer; the other selling his masterpiece for four pounds. But, in the language of Pope, who now reads Cowley? Who that reads Milton does not feel that he is in communion with the noblest of thoughts fitted to inspire men of all time? Neither Wilkes nor Cowley served their generation, nor did they serve God intelligently. Service to one's generation does not consist in defiance, not in defying the tendencies of the generation, like the fanatics of the second century, who defied martyrdom by pulling down the bulletined decrees of the government. Thirty years ago two sets of men attacked the American Republic from opposite sides. Men on one side denounced the national Constitution as a compact with hell, eager to tear it into fragments, because it defended what they regarded as a most accursed institution. On the other side, it was assailed by men who would overthrow the American Republic because it did not defend and uphold this same institution; and God, in His all-wise Providence, by floods of blood, swept away the cause of contention, bringing unspeakable benedictions upon the race. These men did not intelligently serve their own generation. God overruled their madness. So also must be denounced that sort of wealth-getting in our day which throws markets into panic, wrecks railroads, thrusts wasteful nostrums upon the public, and falsely seeks to benefit posterity. People who do such things serve not their generation, but themselves. The humble baker who had his tomb outside of the walls of Rome covered with inscriptions of the implements of his trade, more worthily perpetuated his memory than these. True service to one's generation requires both insight and foresight,— insight to distinguish between eternal principles of truth and error, grasping the principles of right with a firm, intellectual comprehension, and then urging the generation to accept them; foresight to see, and prepare for, the future from afar.

Secondly, Why should we serve humbly and honestly our generation?

An eternal purpose runs through the lengthening centuries, working through each generation its part toward the great consummation. From different points of view men call this fate, or, at one time, eternal decrees, and, at another time, overruling Providence. But name it what you will, it is that which shapes the eternal whole throughout the generations. Many a generation has been false and recreant to its trust, but there is no failure of God's purposes on the earth. There is an eternal will co-ordinating, shaping those purposes. Will you not be one of the workers? The generation that will not serve its appointed end, like the Jews in the wilderness, shall be swept from the face of the earth. Like the polyps building under the sea, each generation prepares the way for the one that is to come after it.

Every generation is composed of an indefinite number of individual units, each individual touching others at innumerable points, through action and interaction, through giving and receiving. So every man, in order to do his appointed work, must give. He who seeks to receive and never give, is like the heedless farmer who never gives back to the soil what he takes from it. Universal nature teaches us a universal and mutual interdependence. The tree of the forest, by its secret alchemy, extracts nutriment from the soil, imbibes nourishment through the pores of its leaves from the air; but it gives back in new forms to the atmosphere what it has absorbed, and through its falling leaves, its decaying branches, and finally by its dead trunk, gives back again what it has extracted from the earth. So every individual should return again to society what he has been gathering from it.

Only through service to his generation, can each individual attain to the highest possible development of himself. As the athlete gets muscle and vigor through struggle with what taxes his strength, so the individual must develop mind, heart, moral energies, through service to his fellowmen, combating prejudice, fighting with evil, defending the good. The finest graces of character, as well as the noblest virtues of soul, are obtainable only through joining with all one's energy in the conflicts of his time in defence and in furtherance of whatever is noble and heroic and beneficent to mankind. No individual, therefore, is ever rounded out into a complete and symmetrical manhood unless he fulfils his obligations to his generation. The finer graces come only from attrition, daily contact with others. The noblest impulses of the soul are developed by helping others; but the best philanthropist is he who says least.

In what specific ways can we serve the generation that now is — we who live in this State of Rhode Island, and in this city of Providence? What are some of our dangers?

Let us observe some of the worst and most dangerous tendencies of our time. There is an all-absorbing passion for gain. In a young man's choice of a profession, the question is asked, "What are the profits of it?" Parents ask the question, "Is it an avenue of wealth?" The whole heart of modern society is inflamed with this passion; every vein of social organism is throbbing with the pulse of this fever. Educated men, above all, should show that there is something higher, nobler, worthier to be sought than mere wealth. Let it be understood that the first object in life is not to acquire wealth, but to help men. It belongs to the educated man to uplift his fellowmen, to be a promoter of character; for the helping of mankind is of more consequence than the helping of one's self.

There is a general disposition on the part of American citizens to surrender the control of their political convictions to the dictation of unscrupulous partisans, the direction and control of votes to what are called rings and political machines. Political parties are necessarily differently marked; they exist and will exist, and it is well that they should; but every self-respecting and thinking man must serve his generation by standing for the right, by contending with vehemence for honesty, for honor, for political integrity. Every man should say, "I will exercise my independence of thought, and woe to the leader who attempts to control my action and my vote! Woe to the man who shall seek to bridle and curb my power of choosing between right and wrong!" We are required in our day, by all that is highest in patriotism, to say, "Whereas I have been intrusted with the privilege of casting a vote, I will cast it for honor, truth, and justice, come what may, whether it results in the disintegration of a political party or not."

There is another danger, and I feel an extreme delicacy in touching upon it, but it should be mentioned. We have a law here in Rhode Island prohibiting the sale of intoxicating liquors. At the beginning of the operation of the law there was an immediate, a marked, a widespread diminution of crime. The law for the time was obeyed. There were indications of purity; there were indications of social order. Every one was rejoiced. There was not, however, a cessation of the private and personal consumption of articles which the law had prohibited. For the supply of this consumption there were importations which speedily became known. Liquors were used by people of prominence in society and on public occasions. The law had not the support of leading citizens. Soon intoxicating liquors were openly exposed for sale. Our city and our State have become disgraced by the public and notorious violators of established law, unspeakably disgraced with drunken persons reeling on our streets. How can the criminal classes be expected to keep the law, when the wealthy and the prominent do not? It is said the law cannot be enforced. Why can't it? Every person, every household, every club (not private clubs alone, but every club) should say, "No liquor to be used here." The common argument, "Why, it has always been sold!" was used long ago. If meat cause my brother to offend, then I will eat no meat; if wine cause my brother to stumble, then I will drink no wine. Heart-rending appeals come up from women and children in pitiful distress; and I beseech every man and every woman, every lover of right, purity, and order to serve their generation by self-denial, by personal abstinence, by themselves respecting the law, giving support to those whose duty it is to enforce it.

[President Robinson now gave his final words of counsel to the gentlemen of the graduating class, who arose as he addressed them. He told them every generation had a right to look to educated men for guidance, for intelligent, helpful service. The discipline and the education which they had received, helped them above the average man to render this help to the generation of which they were a part. He informed them it remained to be seen when they should come back in the recurring years whether they had been of good service in this world. There would be marks upon them plainly discernible, showing whether they had served their generation according to God's purpose.

He next spoke of the perils of the generation. It is an age of transition, when the old things are passing away. The natural science now studied is not the science our fathers studied. Ours is a new science. Not only is there a new science, but a new theology. After speaking of this progress in modern thought and in all departments of life, the President touched upon the opportunities of the present generation, telling the members of the class that they were now parting at the division of the ways. As on the dividing summit of the Rocky Mountains, two drops of water falling near each other separate, one speeding onward to the Atlantic and the other to the Pacific shores, so they were at the parting of ways, and it depended upon their own decisions under Divine guidance what they should make of their lives. He entreated them to keep honor, to keep integrity, to be true to God, to be true to Jesus Christ, who lived and died for them, and who pledged them to be faithful to the end. He implored that the Father would keep them and crown them with the blessing of God and with the approval of all good men.]

GOD GLORIFIED IN CHARACTER.

Let your light so shine before men, that they may see your good works, and glorify your Father which is in heaven.

MATTHEW v. 16.

EVERY human intelligence sheds some light in the world. It may be a light that lights only a household, possibly a hamlet; it may be a light that illuminates nations, and for centuries. The degree and kind of the light depends partly on the degree of intelligence, partly on the ends towards which the intelligence acts. The deeds which are done reveal distinctly the glory or the shame of the ends for which they are done. It is after the style of Oriental imagery that the text speaks of deeds as casting light. Modern thought goes behind this, and fixes its attention on the source of deeds, — character. It is not so much the doing of a man, but the man himself that modern thought takes cognizance of; and character shows either the glory or shame of the sources whence it is derived. The text sets before you the connection between human character and divine glory. I am aware that " the glory of God," — a phrase so often carelessly dropped, — to modern taste, smacks strongly of religious cant. But this old phrase is full of meaning, — as full of meaning and signifying as much to-day as when used by the ancient Hebrew prophet. It is fitting, therefore, on such a day as this, to ask ourselves how human character can be formed so as to glorify that Creative Mind from which all sprang, by which all are sustained, and to which all rational intelligence shall return for account.

There are three ways of looking at character. First, there is the view that regards it as the mere spontaneous outgrowth of inherited or implanted impulses; something moved from within, but affected from without, springing up like a mushroom, and gone in a day. There are plenty of such characters. Another way of looking at character is by architectural imagery. Character is something carefully built up, slowly and steadily rising. Character may be built on a deep, broad substructure, great blocks of truth sunk deep in the human mind. On such a foundation one can rear a magnificent structure which no vicissitudes can shake, no human calamity overturn. Such a one is not formed in an hour or a day, but requires a lifetime. It is formed by earnest thoughts, persistent purposes, under hardships, in spite of temptations, slowly reared as a grand temple. Another more common idea of character is suggested by the origin of the word. It may be regarded as a mere imprint received from environment, or as an imprint not determined solely by environment, but also by our wills controlling and effecting the impression we choose to receive. The Greek word from which "character" is derived means a stamp, then the impress of the stamp, then the strong, abiding impression which the human soul, by inward power, shapes from outward influences. On either of these conceptions you fix your eyes on the inward forces,— thought, purpose, and moral effort. In all cases character depends entirely on a clear perception of life, a clear resolution as to the use to be made of life; on the purpose which a man forms, and towards which he directs his energies.

There can be no impression on anything so unstable as water; there must be a consistency, to determine what kind of an impression is to be received. The question arises, whence do we derive our impressions? There are two great theories of the origin of the universe. Those are called theists who regard the world as the creation of an Omnipotent, Omniscient, and infinitely Benevolent Being. God created the world from an irresistible overflow of benevolence, because He desired to create beings upon which to lavish His goodness. To such an extent is this carried that it is claimed the whole universe is a boundless system to promote satisfaction. Human satisfaction is blessedness. The world teems and produces that man may gather, saying: "We are the little sovereigns; we are the beings for whom the heavens roll, and whom God girds Himself to wait on." The other theory is exactly opposed to this. God in His eternal counsels created the universe for His own ends, His own glory, that we might see His wisdom and glory. Human beings were created to perceive, recognize, and declare His wisdom and glory. This, carried to its utmost extent, lands us in the conception that all beings were created only to set forth the justice and mercy of God. Human happiness is not excluded, but it exists to subserve the Divine ends. It has even been said that a portion of the race is predestined to eternal damnation to illustrate the Divine glory. Each of these theories is an extreme to which we refuse our assent. Yet we may believe that the world exists for the glory of God without accepting the grimness of the latter theory. Human happiness and Divine glory are so intimately connected that we cannot think of one without the other; they cannot be separated.

Grant that this is true, what, then, should be our ruling purpose? We must fix distinctly on an unchanging purpose, that our acts shall have constant regard to the honor and glory of that Being who gave us existence and made it blessed, — a purpose that requires the help of God, and has the service of God as its end. Here we cannot forget how utterly unfitted human beings are to make themselves objects of glory. No man can set himself up to glorify himself without failure. Such is the competition and selfishness of the world that he will find himself thwarted at every step. Only he who loses his life for righteousness' sake shall save it.

No man can reach a position desirable for him to obtain, who does not reach it as the result of the Divine ordering. He is not placed in it simply because mankind sees he is fitted to obtain it. There is no creature who creeps about on the earth who is so despicable as the man who seeks his own aggrandizement and gratification; and no creatures are so mean as the men who seek glory for themselves at the expense of others. But he who looks about him, searching into the world and looking afar, bent on seeking the Divine will which is also seeking him, is sure to find that will, and often at unexpected times and places.

While it may not be true that it is right for a human being to seek glory as his end, it is true that God has the right to seek a special object of glorification. Two distinct thoughts are connected with the idea of glory. The old writers used to speak of essential glory and declarative glory. The essential was that which was inherent in being. God alone has that. The declarative glory is that which makes known His glory, His glorious will. God makes known His purpose to glorify man, and therefore He is glorifying His own ends. So that we can not separate human happiness from Divine glory. To glorify God, therefore, is to declare, to make known His glory. You may ask how a declaration of Divine glory can be made in the world? First of all, by declaring its worth. How we set to work to glorify man! How men glorify military genius with epics! How men glorify holiness with lyrics, as David glorified the holiness of God! There is something to recognize in God. Are not men exalted who ponder on the nature of God, His holiness, His love, His infinite mercies? Do they not thus declare His glory? How are we lifted up and inspired by the contemplation of that majestic character illustrious above all at the Centennial Exposition! How men going to and fro on that busy street in New York look up at the serene bronze face of the statue in front of the Treasury building, and glorify his patriotism! It lifts up every human heart by its dignity, until one is constrained to say, so may I live that my life may be an honor to my country, a sacrifice for the common weal. How infinitely more, when one turns to Christ and hears the cry, " I have finished the work Thou gavest me to do, Father, glorify Thy name!" are we stimulated to all that is best and noblest in life, all that can glorify "our Father" and His Father.

There is no principle of human nature which so elevates the human soul as gratitude. We despise the man whose heart contains envy. Noble characters recognize worth wherever it is, and glorify it. Gratitude to God, the Giver of every good and perfect gift, is our highest glory. He whose wisdom is written all over the heavens and the earth, whose tender mercies temper His resistless judgments, has Himself told us in what a man should glory: "Let him that glorieth glory in this, that he understandeth and knoweth Me; that I am the Lord which exercise loving-kindness, judgment, and righteousness in the earth." Can grateful hearts think of anything more worthy of glory? In a generation like ours, in which we are called on to believe that the course of the world is only a blind progress, blundering on towards human ends, does it not become us to see in this wonderful evolution the Divine glory; to set forth that Divine order which, out of the chaos of the past, has ever more and more manifested forth the glory of God's laws, His justice, and His mercy?

But there is another reason for giving God glory, and why we should not deprive Him of the glory due Him. It is in the power which He has given to man to accomplish great ends. You can recognize this regard for Him in the most imperfect forms. Take Mahomet, who taught his disciples the war cry with which they swept over Eastern Europe, "Allah is Allah." It fired their souls with the thought, that God is *God*, and that He had committed to them the destiny of a people, the power of doing and enforcing His will. It fired their hearts in the midst of conquest. So, in Cromwell's army, we have another and higher example of the power given to men to accomplish great ends. What they were, those old Ironsides, we know. We stigmatize them as self-glorifying Calvinists; but they had conceptions of right, of justice, and of belief in God. And though they had canting men among them, they believed thoroughly that they were fighting, as they truly were, for the glory of God. We know what was in the minds of those who came to our own country. What nerved them but the glory of God? True, they asked for freedom to worship God; but they had also the other thought, — that God had trusted the greatness of His religion to them to defend. So all through history there is to be seen one great unfailing purpose. Is there not a mind there, a divine purpose? What can so exalt human nature as to unite itself to that Divine unchanging Purpose which uplifts, and upholds, and gives victory. Take that noted man of a little more than a century ago, the stern old Calvinist, Samuel Hopkins. Kept on a salary of an almost starvation amount, his thoughts were so filled with the majesty and glory of God that his soul was fired to set it forth. Before him, here in Rhode Island, were men engaged in selling the flesh and blood of slaves. Standing here, he bearded the men in his own congregation, on whom his subsistence depended. There is something heroic in it. Two modern writers, Froude and Bancroft, each wrote a special paper on Calvinism, — a principle as old as human thinking, — wherein they declared that no great movement for three centuries could be traced that had not had this central thought behind it. Never was there a period more fitting to declare it than now. So might we enumerate many another reason why each of us should decide to be guided by, and unite with, that Will by which the world was created and is governed.

Gentlemen of the Graduating Class: Doubtless each one of you has already laid something of the foundation of your future character. Your character has already begun to be formed. Whether upon a foundation of righteousness, love, and truth, God and you alone know. Each one of you, looking into your own heart, may know the kind of character you possess, and whether it is worthy a divine recognition. You have reached a period of reflection and anticipation. Every youth

> " By visions splendid
> Is on his way attended."

Those visions will fade in the coming days as the shades of the prison-house of life close around you. You are coming to see the temptations, trials, vicissitudes, and dangers of life, to see the necessity of calling on high inward principles of action, uniformly, persistently. What is your life to be? Will you forget God, striving to build on a foundation of your own strength with the materials that lie around human souls? Or will you say unto yourselves, "As for me, I seek to honor Him who has set before me my task, who has transformed my soul, and to honor the name He has called me by"? He alone can bring you out of all that can debase, to purity and beauty of character. Be assured that a character formed steadily by daily acts is an indestructible possession. God Almighty, I say it reverently, cannot destroy human character. No fire can burn it, no robber can rob you of it; it is yours forever. But you must build it slowly, steadily. The piercing eyes of man will pronounce a judgment if it is right. But each choice is a crisis. The judgment is not of the hour. God calls you to eternal judgment. Beginning now, a consummation for eternity will be reached at the throne of God. In the final judgment you will say, God's gifts are of God. God help you! God helping you, may you render unto Christ the things that are Christ's, — your acquisitions, your services, yourselves.

www.ingramcontent.com/pod-product-compliance
Lightning Source LLC
Chambersburg PA
CBHW031729230426
43669CB00007B/291